LEGAL ASPECTS OF
Buying, Owning and Selling
A HOME

Daniel L. Johnson

BETTERWAY BOOKS
Cincinnati, Ohio

Cover design by Rick Britton
Typography by Park Lane Associates

96 95 94 93 92   5 4 3 2 1

The purpose of this book is to provide the reader with basic legal
principles and terminology used in the purchase, sale, and use of a
home. This information is intended to be educational in nature. Due
to the local variance of laws, customs, and policies, the material
herein is not to be used or interpreted as a substitute for professional
advice on any specific real estate issue.

Library of Congress Cataloging-in-Publication Data
Johnson, Daniel L.
    Legal aspects of buying, owning, and selling a home / Daniel L.
Johnson.
        p. cm.
    Includes index.
    ISBN 1-55870-246-6 (pbk.) : $12.95
    1. Vendors and purchasers--United States--Popular works. 2. House
buying--United States. 3. House selling--United States. I. Title.
KF665.Z9J64 1992
346.7304'362--dc20
[347.3064362]   92-17181
                                                          CIP

To my wife, Susan, who makes our house a home.

ACKNOWLEDGMENTS Acknowledgment and sincere appreciation go to my secretary and legal assistant, Ruth Christensen, and also my law partner, David Latenser, for their constant support and valuable assistance toward the preparation of this book. I would also like to thank Hilary Swinson for her editorial skills, and Jim Londay for his real estate expertise.

Contents

Introduction

Our builder is several months behind schedule. Is there anything we can do to speed things up?

Are my home utility bills deductible as a business expense, since I repair lawnmowers part-time in my basement?

We are trying to sell our home without a real estate broker. Should we agree to sell if a buyer wants to use a land installment sales contract?

During my practice of law, I have heard these types of questions on a regular basis. All too often, the homeowner or home buyer has not adequately protected or promoted his legal interests, usually to his economic detriment.

My purpose in writing this book is twofold: to allow the home buyer to understand the basic legalities of the purchase process and to create an awareness of the general principles of law that affect him as a homeowner.

I believe that all homeowners need to have a strong appreciation of the law of residential real estate. An understanding of the topics and concepts in this book can, over the years, potentially save the homeowner thousands of dollars that might otherwise be lost during the purchase transaction or in avoidable legal disputes. Real estate brokers and other real estate professionals would also be well-served by reviewing the material in this book.

In sum, this book is designed to provide the reader with a comprehensive, long-term legal guide to anyone buying, selling, or owning a home.

The pronouns *he*, *his*, and *him* as used in this book are not intended to denote masculine gender exclusively, rather they are utilized to avoid awkward or redundant grammar.

1

The Parties to the Purchase: Their Roles, Duties, and Obligations

The sale or purchase of a home involves many players. In addition to a buyer and a seller, the transaction often includes the services of brokers, attorneys, lenders, appraisers, and title insurance companies.

All these individuals or entities have specific roles, duties, and obligations throughout the transaction. The purpose of this chapter is to explore these various roles so you can understand how to protect your interests and participate effectively throughout the purchase process.

THE SELLER In almost all home purchases, the buyer works either directly with the seller or with the seller's real estate broker. The following section discusses the advantages and disadvantages of each situation.

For Sale by Owner In a *for sale by owner* home, the buyer or buyer's representative deals directly with the seller. One of the disadvantages of this, depending upon the mindset of the particular seller, is that the seller may believe that his home is worth more than market conditions warrant. This makes the buyer's goal of trying to obtain a fair purchase price much more difficult than might be the case if the seller were represented by a broker.

Offsetting this disadvantage is the fact that the seller is not obligated to pay a broker's commission upon the sale of the home. He therefore may be willing to reduce the sale price of the home.

Listed Homes Most homes are sold after the owner has listed his home with a real estate broker. A complete discussion of the types of listing agreements a broker and a homeowner can enter into is included later in this chapter. Once a home is listed, a potential buyer must deal with the listing broker in trying to reach an agreement to purchase the home. Under most types of listing agreements, even if the buyer purchases the home direct from the owner without broker participation or assistance, the listing broker is still entitled to receive a commission.

Estate, Foreclosure, and Trustee Sales

If an individual dies owning a home, his estate is *probated*, that is, his assets are sold and distributed to his heirs. A court typically appoints an individual, commonly called an *executor* or a *personal representative*, to close out the affairs of the deceased. The deed to the home remains in the decedent's name, but the executor of the estate is granted the power to sell the home unless otherwise provided for in the will or directed by the court.

There is no inherent disadvantage to the buyer in purchasing a home from the executor of an estate. In fact, a buyer can sometimes get advantageous sale terms since the executor has an obligation to complete the affairs of the estate as efficiently and quickly as possible, as long as a reasonable price for the home is received.

The buyer's attorney should conduct a search of the public records and court documents to determine that the executor does indeed have the power to sell the home and that there are no unknown *encumbrances* or *title defects* to the property, including potential claims or *liens* by the deceased's heirs or creditors.

In the event of a *tax sale, mortgage foreclosure sale,* or *judgment sale,* the local sheriff or constable has the power to sell real estate. This power is exercised through various means. If delinquent taxes on the home have not been paid, or when a mortgage has not been paid and the lender has conducted foreclosure proceedings, or if a particular creditor has obtained a judgment lien through the court process, these individuals or entities have the legal right to collect what is owed by forcing a sale of the debtor's home.

In most jurisdictions, a buyer purchasing a home at a sheriff's sale is not necessarily obtaining good and valid title. Extra care should be made to determine that no outside interests will hinder the buyer at such a sale. Further, most jurisdictions provide a *right of redemption* that allows a foreclosed owner of the home the legal right (for a certain period of time after the sale) to redeem title to the home if the past taxes, mortgage arrearages, or judgment amounts are paid. Rights of homeowners in these situations vary widely throughout the country, and a buyer should be aware of applicable local laws before attempting to purchase a home at this type of sale.

A buyer can also purchase real estate from a *trustee* by way of a *deed of trust*. A trustee is an individual who, through a deed of trust previously executed by the homeowner, has in effect foreclosed on the home and is now selling the property in an attempt to recoup the lender's losses. As with a sheriff's sale, an individual purchasing a home directly from a trustee in a deed of trust sale should assure himself that no outside encumbrances exist, which may hamper his future use or title rights. Again, local laws vary greatly in this area, and a thorough understanding of them is recommended prior to buying a home in this fashion.

Power of Attorney Another instance in which the buyer may be dealing with a third party rather than the seller is through a *power of attorney*. A purchase through a power of attorney is valid if an individual who owns a home has given another individual a general power of attorney, or a power of attorney directly authorizing someone else to sell the owner's real estate. However, if the power of attorney is legally defective, the purchase may not be valid. You should have the power of attorney reviewed by your attorney prior to the sale.

Corporate Sales If a buyer is purchasing a home owned by a corporation, the individual who executes both the purchase agreement and the deed on behalf of the corporate seller must have the proper legal authority to act on the corporation's behalf. This is usually accomplished by means of a *corporate resolution*, a document signed by the corporate board of directors either ratifying or authorizing the sale.

A buyer should always require that any corporate sale be accompanied by such documentation. Without it, the corporation may have the legal option to declare the sale void. It is not necessary that the board of directors actually execute the purchase agreement or deed, but only approve the sale. A corporate officer, such as the president or the vice president, can sign these documents.

The Seller's Responsibility to the Buyer A homeowner attempting to sell his home has legal obligations to prospective and actual buyers. Perhaps most important (and most obvious) is that the seller must deal honestly with any potential buyer. What does this really mean? Does the seller have a responsibility always to inform the buyer of the complete condition of the home, or is it up to the buyer to protect himself? How much information regarding the status of the home must legally be disclosed?

Intentional Misrepresentation First, recognize that any fraud committed by the homeowner or his real estate broker can be grounds for the buyer to either *rescind* (legally cancel) the purchase agreement or sue for any damages incurred due to the fraud. Fraud in real estate transactions is defined as affirmatively making a false representation, or failing to disclose facts that should have been brought to the attention of the buyer by the seller or the seller's agent.

Intentional misrepresentations are fairly easy to recognize. For instance, if the homeowner states to the buyer that the home was constructed of a certain material (and it obviously was not), or that the furnace and air conditioner had been replaced recently (and they were not), or that the home had recently been successfully treated for termites (when it had not), the buyer would have a basis for a lawsuit due to the seller's intentional misrepresentation.

The issue is always this: Did the homeowner deliberately misrepresent a fact upon which the buyer had reasonably relied and which caused the buyer injury? If such a misrepresentation occurred, and the buyer has suffered a loss because of it, the seller and possibly his broker can be held legally responsible.

Negligent Misrepresentation

More difficult, however, is the concept of *negligent misrepresentation* or *negative fraud*. Many courts have ruled that a seller of real estate has a duty to disclose certain *material defects* known to him and to advise the buyer of these defects. This is the rule even if the buyer does not inquire about such defects. The question, of course, then becomes, what specific material facts does the homeowner have to disclose?

Dangerous defects. The types of defects that must be disclosed can be broken down into two categories. First are the so-called *dangerous defects*. Homeowners and their brokers must disclose any type of defect that may make the property dangerous to the buyer, who would otherwise be unaware of the defect.

For instance, if a home's well water is unfit for consumption, the homeowner must disclose this fact to the buyer. If the wiring in the home is faulty or known to cause electrical malfunctioning, this also must be disclosed to the buyer.

Latent defects. A homeowner trying to sell his home must also disclose any *latent defects*. These types of defects are defined as a material defect in the home that is not readily apparent to the buyer. The classic example would be the water-in-the-basement situation.

Here, the buyer inspects the home on a sunny day and is unable to determine whether water would leak into the basement if it was raining. No other evidence of water damage being apparent to the buyer, the buyer assumes that no water problem exists. Later, after the home has been purchased, it is discovered that there had been extensive water damage in the basement before the sale. This type of defect would be termed a latent defect, one that is not readily or apparently discernible by the buyer upon reasonable inspection.

If the defect is latent, the defect must be disclosed by the seller regardless of whether the buyer inquires about any such condition. Generally, if a lay person would not be able to discover that a defect existed, the seller is obligated to inform the buyer of such a defect. This assumes that the defect is material in nature; that is, one that a reasonable person would consider as a factor in deciding whether or not to purchase the home. Most latent defects have to do with the structure of the home.

It should be mentioned that the law in this particular area has recently expanded. In some states, real estate brokers have been held liable for not disclosing an unknown defect to the buyer, even though the broker was not made aware of the defect by the homeowner. To state it another way, the broker has a *duty to discover* whether any type of latent defect does exist, and, if so, to disclose the defect to the buyer. If the broker fails to discover and disclose any existing latent defect, both the homeowner and the broker could be held liable for any resulting damages to the buyer.

Remember, there is nothing illegal about a homeowner selling a home with latent defects as long as these defects are properly disclosed to the buyer. As a practical matter, however, it is advisable for a seller to include a clause in the purchase agreement specifically stating that all such latent defects have been disclosed (if in fact they have), even if verbal disclosures have been previously made.

"As Is" Purchases It is worth noting that most home purchase agreements contain an *as is* provision. This provision usually states that the buyer is purchasing the home as it exists, without any warranties by the seller. Often the purchase agreement further states that the buyer has had a reasonable opportunity to inspect the home and is not relying upon the seller's or seller's agent's representations, or lack thereof. It has been held by most courts that these types of disclaimers in the purchase agreement do not remove the liability of the homeowner or his broker for fraud or negligent misrepresentation.

Seller/Listing Broker Responsibility A homeowner must truthfully answer all inquiries his listing broker may have concerning the condition of the home. If the homeowner knows of a particular latent defect and deliberately does not inform his broker of it, in some states the broker would have a legal defense to any liability claim based upon the buyer's allegations of negligent misrepresentation or fraud.

The flip side of this, however, is that the listing broker should always inquire of the seller as to any potential latent defects in the home. The failure of the broker to make these inquiries may result in his being held liable if the buyer incurs damages because of such an undisclosed defect.

Patent Defects *Patent defects* are defects that are readily apparent to the buyer. The homeowner is not legally required to disclose patent defects. A crumbling front porch, outwardly apparent cracks in the foundation, standing water, or visible evidence of water damage in the basement are examples of patent defects. Because notice of such types of defects is considered legally apparent, the seller has no duty to point them out.

Buyer's Question Rule An exception to the aforementioned latent defect/patent defect disclosure standards is the *buyer's question* rule. If the buyer has asked a specific question about any aspect of the home, the seller or his broker must answer the question truthfully. More important, if the situation inquired about should subsequently change, the seller must immediately notify the buyer of the change in condition. If he does not do so, the buyer may have a legal basis for canceling or rescinding the purchase.

For example, let's say a buyer happens to inquire about a particular crack in the foundation, and the homeowner states that the crack has been there for years and it has not caused any damage whatsoever to the structure of the home. Then, a few weeks prior to closing, a portion of the home tilts several inches, apparently due to a worsening of the crack in the foundation. The homeowner must update his response to the buyer. That is, if the homeowner once answered truthfully, and the condition involved subsequently and materially changes, the homeowner must immediately notify the buyer.

Implied Obligations of the Seller

The purchase agreement for a home determines the written obligations the homeowner has concerning the sale. In addition, the seller has duties that will be implied by law regardless of the express terms of the agreement.

If no mention of a specific closing date is made in the purchase agreement, it is implied that a reasonable period of time is to pass to enable the buyer to procure the funds to pay the seller. How long is a reasonable period of time? It depends upon the facts; however, sixty days is typical if the buyer needs to obtain a loan commitment prior to buying the home.

If the purchase agreement fails to mention that the homeowner is to transfer the deed when the buyer has obtained the money to purchase the home, the seller must execute and forward the deed to the buyer when the buyer indicates he has the funds to close. Any delay in transferring the deed constitutes a breach by the seller of this implied duty.

Also implied in every real estate purchase agreement is the duty of the seller to vacate the premises once the home has been sold. Even though not technically a trespasser, if after the deed is transferred the seller remains in the home, he is in breach of the implied condition of the purchase agreement with regard to vacating the premises upon transfer of ownership. The buyer would then be able to pursue the seller legally for any damages he might incur.

Naturally, if agreed upon by the parties, the date of possession can occur before or after the day title is actually transferred. This type of arrangement is discussed in Chapter 5, concerning early-late occupancy agreements.

Usually after a real estate purchase agreement is signed, several weeks pass during which time the buyer attempts to procure the money to pay the seller in exchange for the deed to the home. During this period of time, it is the seller's responsibility to keep the home in good repair and maintain the property in the same condition as when the purchase agreement was entered into.

Should the premises fall into severe disrepair or be damaged to an extent that the seller cannot repair the premises to their original condition, the seller will be in breach of the purchase agreement, and the buyer may have a legal basis for refusing to honor the contract.

Also, if a third party should damage the home subsequent to the date of the purchase agreement, the seller does have the obligation (and will be given the opportunity) to repair the property and keep the buyer bound to the terms of the purchase agreement. It is incumbent on the seller, however, to make all necessary repairs on a timely basis.

Even though the obligations of the seller with regard to timely closing, vacating the premises, and maintaining the property are implied in the purchase agreement, it is good practice to state these obligations specifically in the written agreement itself, so as to avoid any misunderstanding or avoidable legal expense.

THE BUYER Despite what you have just read concerning all the duties the seller has to the buyer, the responsibility of the buyer is largely toward himself. The concept of *caveat emptor* governs the buyer's legal position.

Caveat Emptor *Caveat emptor* is a legal term meaning *let the buyer beware*. Practically speaking, this means that, for the most part, no one is going to protect the buyer's interests except the buyer.

For example, the seller may state in the purchase agreement that the home's furnace, air conditioning, and plumbing will be in good working order at the time of closing. Only a naive buyer would take these assurances at face value. A prudent buyer has a common sense duty to check the mechanical workings of the home to make sure that they are in acceptable condition.

It is possible that the buyer may be able to sue the seller for damages if these items were not in the condition promised at closing. However, not only would the buyer be faced with potentially unnecessary legal expense, he may also encounter the practical difficulty of proving that the problem existed prior to closing rather than after the buyer took possession of the home.

As discussed in the previous section, only certain types of defects need to be disclosed to the buyer. Accordingly, the buyer should always inspect the home to his satisfaction, regardless of any assertions or lack of notification by the seller or the seller's broker. Only in this manner can the buyer truly protect himself from future disputes or legal problems arising from undisclosed defects in the home.

Buyer's Responsibilities The buyer does have certain responsibilities and obligations inherent in the purchase of a home. First of all, the buyer is obligated to disclose his true financial status. What this means is that the buyer cannot fraudulently hold himself out to be more wealthy or have more financial backing than is actually the case.

If a purchase agreement is entered into, and the seller of the home has relied upon certain fraudulent assertions the buyer has made about his financial condition, it allows the seller to terminate the contract legally.

This rule exists because purchase agreements are often entered into contingent upon the buyer obtaining specific financing necessary to purchase the home, or, in the alternative, the buyer will be able to purchase the property without having to obtain a loan. If the buyer has lied or misled the seller with regard to his financial condition, it can easily keep the sale from closing.

The potential home buyer may also be in the process of trying to sell his current home. If this is the case, the buyer includes in the purchase agreement a statement that his legal obligation to purchase the home only becomes binding if he is successful in selling his existing home. This contingency causes the seller to rely on the buyer to sell his current home and, during the period when the buyer is attempting to sell his existing home, the seller is effectively removing his home from the market with regard to other potential buyers. Thus, the buyer has the legal responsibility to take all necessary steps in attempting to sell his current home.

It is obvious that a homeowner should think twice before entering into a purchase agreement with such a contingency. Even though a purchase agreement has been signed, the buyer is not legally obligated to close unless the buyer sells his existing home. If the seller agrees to such a contingency, a limit on the amount of time that the buyer has to sell his home should be placed in the purchase agreement.

True identity. Another inherent obligation a buyer has in a residential real estate purchase agreement is to disclose his *true identity*. What this means is that the seller has the right to know who he is dealing with because that may have an effect on the negotiations of the purchase price and the terms of the agreement. If, after a purchase agreement is entered into, the homeowner learns that the buyer was in fact an agent or a front for another individual or entity, the homeowner may have legal grounds for refusing to sell.

This *true identity rule* exists to negate any disadvantage the seller may be placed in by the buyer using a third party to conduct his dealings. This rule can also come into play if the buyer is in agreement with a third party who ends up purchasing the home with the express purpose of immediately turning around and selling it to another buyer. Of course, the seller must prove that he was damaged in some respect, such as selling the home for a lesser amount than if he had known the buyer's true identity.

As a corollary to this rule, be aware that in most states a real estate broker must disclose his status as a broker to anyone with whom he is having dealings or negotiations regarding the sale of real estate, including his own. This rule allows for disclosure of the broker's expertise so as not to take advantage of an unaware buyer.

It is not unusual for the purchase agreement to have a contingency clause in which the buyer must obtain a loan to enable him to make the purchase. If the loan is not obtained, the buyer is not obligated to purchase the home. Most purchase agreements state a certain period of time in which the buyer must obtain the loan. If the buyer has not obtained a loan commitment from a lender within that stated period of time, the homeowner is free to sell the home to anyone else because the buyer has not met the terms of the contingency in the purchase agreement. In most cases, the purchase agreement provides for the return of the buyer's *earnest money deposit* if he is unable to obtain the loan. This is a required aspect of any purchase agreement contingent upon Veterans Administration or Federal Housing Administration financing.

A buyer must make a good faith effort to procure necessary financing, if this is a contingency in the purchase agreement. This means that the buyer must take all reasonable steps necessary to procure the loan, and, usually, if the buyer is turned down for one loan at otherwise acceptable rates and terms, he must try again with at least one other lender before the buyer's duty to obtain financing is extinguished and the purchase agreement rendered void. If the buyer does not take reasonable steps to obtain the necessary loan to purchase the home, the seller may have a cause of action against the buyer for any damages incurred. At the least, the purchase agreement will no longer be binding on the seller.

When the buyer does obtain a loan to purchase the home, he has the implied obligation of closing. That is, if the buyer does obtain a loan commitment from a lender to enable the buyer to make the purchase, the buyer must take advantage of that loan and proceed toward closing. If the buyer does not proceed toward a timely closing once the purchase funds are available, the seller may have a legal cause of action against the buyer for all resulting damages.

REAL ESTATE BROKERS

In most areas of the country, real estate brokers are involved in the bulk of residential real estate sales. A real estate broker is an individual who has obtained a state license to sell, transfer, or lease real estate on behalf of another, for compensation. Most real estate brokers are governed by certain state statutes and rules that regulate their professional conduct.

Many states have both real estate brokers and real estate salespeople. The general difference is that a real estate broker is presumed to have a higher level of expertise and is allowed to govern or monitor the actions and transactions of the real estate salespeople working for him. The duties and obligations of a real estate broker or real estate salesperson, however, are basically the same when dealing with the public. Whenever the term *broker* is used in this text, it includes real estate brokers and real estate salespeople or agents.

Listing Brokers

With some exceptions, most brokers are employed by, and have an obligation to, the seller. The broker whose name appears on the "For Sale" sign is called the *listing broker*. The listing broker enters into a contract with the owner of the home, in which the owner has given that broker the authority to use his expertise in attempting to sell the home at a certain price.

With few exceptions, the listing broker will only be paid if the home sells. When and if the home does sell, the amount of compensation to the listing broker is typically a percentage of the sale price. This percentage generally ranges from five to eight percent. There is no minimum or maximum with regard to the amount of commission that a listing broker can receive, and this figure is a matter of negotiation between the homeowner and the listing broker.

Listing Agreements   There are different types of listing agreements. Probably the least common type is a *non-exclusive* or *open* listing agreement. This listing agreement is a contract between a homeowner and a broker, whereby the broker will be paid a commission based upon the sale price of the home if and when that particular broker initiates a series of events that causes the home to sell. This type of listing agreement does not prohibit the homeowner from entering into similar listing agreements with other brokers, who would earn the commission if they caused the sale to occur. Furthermore, if the homeowner sells his home totally through his own efforts, no commission would be earned by any broker. For obvious reasons, these types of listing contracts are generally not preferred by brokers.

As a seller, you might think that an open listing would be to your advantage. You may believe that by entering into many open listing contracts, you would have many brokers working simultaneously in an attempt to sell the home. In reality, no brokers are working for you since all the brokers realize that their chances of earning the sales commission through an open listing are very low and, hence, little or no effort will be given to locating an acceptable buyer.

Another type of listing agreement is the *exclusive agency* listing agreement. This type of listing is entered into between the homeowner and a broker and gives only that broker the authority to sell the home. This type of listing requires all other brokers to work through the listing broker when showing the home or submitting offers.

The homeowner does retain the right to sell his home on his own, and, if the homeowner should do so, he would not be liable to the listing broker for any commission. Understand that the homeowner must show that it was solely his efforts that caused the home to sell. Otherwise, the listing broker is entitled to the sales commission. Generally, if the listing broker can prove that something he did caused the buyer to become interested or eventually to purchase the home, then the broker is most likely entitled to the commission if the home ultimately sells to that particular buyer.

The third and most common type of listing agreement is the *exclusive right to sell* listing. (There is an example of this type of listing agreement in the Appendix.) This listing is entered into between the homeowner and the broker, giving the broker the exclusive and sole right to sell the home for a certain period of time. As with the exclusive agency listing, no other brokers can legally be employed to sell the home during that period of time. More important, the homeowner must pay a commission to the listing broker even if the sale occurs entirely due to the owner's efforts. That is, once the exclusive right to sell agreement has been executed, the homeowner has to pay the agreed upon commission to the listing broker if the home is sold, regardless of whether the eventual buyer was procured with or without any effort or assistance by the listing broker.

Accordingly, as a practical matter, if a homeowner is aware of a buyer who may be interested in his home, he should make his listing broker aware of this fact so as to omit such a potential buyer from the exclusive right to sell listing agreement. This is called an *exclusion*. There is nothing illegal or unethical about a homeowner excluding potential buyers at the time that the listing agreement is entered into. It serves to protect the seller from having to pay a commission to the listing broker when the buyer would have purchased the home regardless of whether it was listed with the broker.

Most state administrative laws require that the listing agreement be in writing and that a copy of the listing agreement be provided to the homeowner. The specific rate of commission that is earned upon the sale of the home must also be agreed upon and stated in the listing agreement. Most listing agreements state what powers the broker will have, such as being able to conduct open houses, placing a "For Sale" sign in the yard, advertising the home through a local multiple listing service, and so on.

There is no maximum or minimum time that a listing agreement needs to be in effect. Most brokers want the greatest amount of time possible to sell the home, while the seller may want to keep the time at a minimum so that he will not be locked into a contract with a particular broker who may not be doing an adequate job in trying to sell the home. A standard time frame for a listing agreement is in the neighborhood of sixty to 120 days.

The Agency Relationship As previously mentioned, once a broker has entered into a listing agreement with a homeowner, that broker and the salespeople working for him have made themselves the lawful agent of the homeowner. Once this *agency relationship* is created, certain duties and obligations from the broker to the seller come into play.

First and foremost, the listing broker has a *fiduciary duty* to the seller during the term of the listing agreement. This means that the broker must put the seller's interest above his own in attempting to market the home, and he must represent the seller within the parameters of the sale. Stated another way, the listing broker must protect and maximize the seller's position in attempting to sell the home. Once this fiduciary duty takes effect, the seller has the legal right to rely upon his broker to promote his interests by procuring the highest possible sale price for the home, as quickly as possible.

Included within this concept of fiduciary duty are three main rules. First, the listing broker must disclose all information to his seller with regard to the sale of the home. This means that: the broker must forward *all* offers to the seller; the broker must advise the seller of the true and correct identity of any potential buyer who is making an offer; and the broker must keep his seller informed as to any pertinent information or relevant factors that may have an effect on the seller's decision to sell.

Stated simply, the broker acts as a piece of glass. Any information that comes to him should pass, without distortion, directly to the homeowner so as to allow him immediate access to all information that may be pertinent in deciding when to sell, whom to sell to, and at what price to sell. Under no circumstances should the broker ever sift or withhold information that pertains to the sale of the home. This is true even if the broker honestly believes that the information involved may not be of interest to the seller. The homeowner is relying on the broker to forward all information to him, and it is up to the homeowner, not the broker, to decide what is and what is not important with regard to the transaction.

The reverse of this is also true. The broker cannot divulge any information to a potential buyer that could prejudice the seller's position. Assume that a home is listed for $84,000 and the homeowner has advised his listing broker that he would accept an offer of $80,000 but nevertheless wants to try and obtain $84,000. A potential buyer asks the broker if the homeowner would take $82,000. The broker replies: "Sure, in fact he already told me he would accept $80,000." If the broker did answer this way, he would be in violation of his fiduciary duty to the seller. The broker could only reply that $84,000 is the listed price. He cannot indicate in any way that the seller would accept less.

A second duty of a listing broker is to account to the seller for all proceeds with regard to the sale of the home. The broker cannot use any money as his own that he may have access to because of his relationship with the seller. He must keep any such money (such as escrow deposits, earnest money, etc.) separate and distinct from his general use funds. If a *commingling of funds* does occur, the broker is in breach of his fiduciary duty and the seller may have a legal cause of action against the broker. At the least, the listing broker would have no right to any commission that would otherwise be earned.

Third, the listing broker must obey his seller. The broker has a level of knowledge and expertise to advise the seller regarding the sale of the home, but under no circumstances may the broker disobey or disregard what the seller decides to do.

For instance, if the broker is attempting to list the home for $100,000, and the homeowner will not list it for anything less than $140,000, under no circumstances may the broker list it for anything less than $140,000. Of course, the broker may refuse to enter into the listing, but once the listing has been created, he cannot disregard what the seller has directed and must abide by his seller's decisions. This includes the acceptance or rejection of any offer on the home.

Duties to Buyers Does the broker who has a listing contract with a seller have any duty to a buyer or potential buyer? No fiduciary duty to the buyer exists if the broker is listing the home. This does not mean that the listing broker can deceive the buyer or fraudulently misrepresent any conditions of the home.

As already discussed in this chapter, a buyer does have certain rights with regard to dealing with the seller or the seller's agent, and these rights revolve around the seller dealing fairly and honestly with the buyer. However, understand that a listing broker who has a fiduciary duty to the homeowner cannot inform a potential buyer of any particular circumstance of the seller or the home that would compromise the seller's position. (One exception to this is the aforementioned rules concerning latent or dangerous defects.) If such a disclosure is made without the seller's express permission, and the buyer has taken advantage of this information to the seller's detriment, the listing broker has breached his duty of confidentiality and not met his fiduciary duty to the homeowner.

For example, assume that a potential buyer inquires why the homeowner is selling his home. This listing broker replies: "Oh, he needs cash in a hurry. In fact, he's pretty desperate for a sale." This type of information could cause a buyer to offer less for the home than if this information had not been divulged by the listing broker. The broker has almost certainly violated his fiduciary duty toward the homeowner and as a result forfeited his commission. The broker could also be held liable for any consequent damages incurred by the seller.

Since no agency relationship exists between the listing broker and the buyer, the buyer should always understand and appreciate that the broker is attempting to sell the home at the highest possible price, and the buyer is merely a customer, not a client, of the listing broker.

Cooperative Brokers Often other brokers who are not directly connected with the listing broker will be involved in the sale of a home. A broker may be in the process of showing various homes to a potential buyer, and informing that buyer of how much he could obtain as far as a loan is concerned, the different types of financing available, and so on, but this type of broker is not considered a legal agent of the buyer. If he were, all the fiduciary duties and obligations previously mentioned with regard to a seller and a listing broker would come into play.

Rather, these types of brokers are known as *cooperative brokers* or *sub-brokers*. They are in effect an extension of the listing broker and have the same legal duties and obligations to the seller that the listing broker has. The buyer should always remember that, with few exceptions, any broker involved has his legal duty to the homeowner and will not disclose any information that would compromise the seller's position.

This does not mean that cooperative brokers can act dishonestly toward the buyer. But the buyer should be aware that the broker's prime focus is to obtain the highest selling price possible, while obviously the buyer is trying to obtain the lowest possible purchase price. The buyer should consider himself a customer and, as with any customer, protect his own interest by making all reasonable inquiries of the product (the home) being purchased.

The commission agreed upon in the listing agreement between the listing broker and the seller determines how these cooperative brokers are paid. Usually a percentage of the listing broker's commission goes to any cooperative broker involved in the sale. How much of the commission the cooperative broker receives depends on local practice.

Buyer Agency There are, however, circumstances in which a broker can act as the legal agent to a potential buyer. As such, that broker has a fiduciary duty to the *buyer*. A broker who is legally representing the buyer is obligated to protect that buyer's interest throughout the sale and has a strict allegiance and duty to his buyer to procure the lowest purchase price possible. A *buyer's broker* does not have any fiduciary duty to the seller.

Generally, a broker only represents a buyer in this way when a formal agreement is created establishing buyer representation. There have been situations, however, where the courts have ruled that a broker does represent a buyer even though no such agreement existed. This usually occurred when the broker committed certain acts or stated certain things that, in the court's opinion, allowed the buyer to reasonably believe that the broker was his agent.

In most cases, a buyer's broker has to be compensated directly by the buyer and not by the homeowner or listing broker. Since no fiduciary duty exists between the buyer's broker and the homeowner, the seller is normally not willing to compensate the buyer's broker. Generally, most home buyers are unwilling to pay a separate fee to be legally represented by a broker, and instead rely on the seller to compensate the brokers involved.

ATTORNEYS

The purchase of a home is often the largest economic transaction in which a person is ever involved. It is estimated that most people buy or sell a home only two or three times during their lives. They cannot be expected to understand how the purchase procedure is fully effectuated, including any legal rights or responsibilities entailed in the process. Thus, attorneys are often used to protect and promote the legal rights of the parties.

An attorney can be hired for two types of representation in a real estate sale. He can be hired to perform a specific task, such as drafting a purchase agreement or clearing up a particular type of title defect, or he can be hired for general representation of the buyer or the seller, or possibly the lender.

Attorneys and Sellers

When an attorney represents the seller of a home, his task is somewhat less complicated than if he were representing the buyer. The seller is primarily concerned with obtaining the agreed upon purchase price. If there are no defects in the title to the home, the seller's attorney has a relatively easy task. He generally sees that the deed is in acceptable form to the buyer at closing, and that the seller receives the agreed upon purchase price.

If, however, a title search discloses a lien or an encumbrance on the home that needs to be removed prior to closing, the attorney for the seller is generally responsible for removing this *cloud on the title*.

For example, if the home had at one time been owned by two individuals and one of them had since died and his estate had never been probated, a state's inheritance tax laws will often have not been satisfied, thus creating a lien on the home. If the deceased is still one of the named owners of the home, that individual will obviously not be able to transfer his interest at the time of closing. Consequently, the seller's attorney will have to proceed with a probate or estate proceeding so as to remove these defects in the *chain of title*.

If there are any judgments against the seller, in most jurisdictions these judgments will constitute a lien on any real estate held in the seller's name. These judgments will have to be removed by paying off the judgment creditor, at which time a *satisfaction* or *release* will need to be filed with the court so as to create public notice that the judgment lien has been extinguished. It is often the attorney for the seller who must determine the basis for the judgment lien, contact the appropriate party, and do what is necessary to have the lien extinguished prior to closing.

Many states provide that if a homeowner has a continuing child support obligation, this constitutes an automatic lien on any real estate in the name of the child support obligor. This being the case, a special court release on the piece of property being sold must be obtained prior to closing so that the buyer will not have the child support lien on the title to the home he is purchasing. It is the seller's attorney who will have to obtain this release prior to closing.

Aside from these typical specific duties, the seller's attorney often works with the brokers so as to allow the transaction to proceed toward closing on a timely basis. If the types of problems mentioned above arise, however, it is the attorney for the seller who will have to act quickly and efficiently to make sure that the closing is not delayed.

Attorneys and Buyers   An attorney who represents a home buyer usually has more responsibility than if he is representing the seller. All the aspects of the purchase should be reviewed and considered by the attorney for the buyer prior to closing. After closing, the buyer has lost much of his economic leverage, and any recourse is more difficult (and expensive) to obtain should a problem be discovered.

A buyer's attorney is involved in reviewing the title to the home. This usually means examining the *abstract* or *title insurance binder* to determine present ownership of the home and to discern whether any break in the chain of title exists. Also, the buyer's attorney can discover if any third parties have an interest in the home that the seller is not going to be able to remove by closing.

Any aspect of the title to the home that the title insurance company is not willing to insure should be specifically discussed with the buyer prior to closing so as to make the buyer aware of these potentially unacceptable title defects. Title insurance is discussed in more detail in later chapters.

The attorney for the buyer should also take steps to advise the buyer if any possible *encroachments* exist on the home's boundary lines. Often, an examination of a plat map or land surveyor's certificate is in order. In residential real estate, however, a review of the actual site should be made by the buyer or the buyer's attorney to discover any potential encroachments, such as a misplaced fence, driveway, or the like.

In many areas, the most efficient and inexpensive way of accomplishing this is to have a licensed surveyor provide the buyer a *situational survey*, which will disclose any such encroachment and, if none is found, provide the buyer with a written guarantee of the home's permanent boundary lines.

If any unpaid taxes, judgment liens, or other types of involuntary title defects exist against the seller, it is the attorney for the buyer who should be satisfied that all these defects are cured prior to closing. If they are not, the buyer could be purchasing a defective title, and a third party may have an interest in the home, which would undoubtedly lead to future legal problems for the buyer.

If the buyer being represented by an attorney is having difficulties obtaining the necessary loan to purchase the home due to poor credit history, the buyer's attorney will sometimes work with the lender to remove any objectionable judgments or negative credit history items that the buyer may have, so as to allow the lender to make the loan.

For example, in some areas of the country lenders require that any child support liens of the buyer be placed in an *inferior position* to the lender's security interest. This is done to enhance the security of the lender. It is the buyer's attorney's job to see that the buyer's child support payment obligation is legally subordinated to the security interest of the lender.

Since most buyers must obtain a loan to procure the purchase price, the buyer's attorney should review the loan documentation. This typically involves a *promissory note* and a mortgage or deed of trust. Although the lender is required to disclose all pertinent aspects of the loan to the buyer at or prior to closing, the attorney for the buyer should review these documents and make the buyer aware of the consequences and ramifications of the financial obligation the buyer is undertaking.

The buyer's attorney should also make the buyer aware of what will happen if he defaults on the loan, and what rights the buyer may have if a potential default does occur. In this way, the buyer is entering into the entire transaction—both the purchase of the home and obtaining the loan—with a clear understanding of his legal rights and obligations.

To allow the attorney to protect either the buyer's or the seller's interests, all documents pertaining to the transaction (including negotiations and relevant verbal commitments) should be forwarded directly from the client to the attorney. If the seller or the buyer refrains from giving his attorney all the information needed, it will be difficult for the attorney to safeguard his client's position in the sale, which is undoubtedly why the attorney was hired in the first place.

Occasionally, a buyer and a seller will request that one attorney handle the legalities of the sale on both their behalfs. As has been seen, the buyer and seller generally have different concerns, requirements, and duties. Hence, it is nearly impossible for one attorney to represent both the buyer and the seller in the same transaction. An attorney who attempts to do so is probably not representing either party effectively.

LENDERS Most buyers are unable to pay the entire purchase price of a home without a loan from a bank, savings and loan, or other type of institutional lender. After satisfying itself that the buyer is a good credit risk, the lender provides the necessary funds to the buyer and, as security for the loan, obtains an interest in the home being purchased.

The lender's security interest usually takes one of two forms: a mortgage or a deed of trust. The similarities and differences of a mortgage and a deed of trust are discussed in Chapter 3. Recognize, however, that these are different devices that the lender may use in obtaining the security necessary for it to be willing to loan the money to the buyer. Generally, if the buyer stops making the necessary repayment to the lender, the lender has the legal right to foreclose on the mortgage or enforce the deed of trust and eventually take title to the home away from the buyer.

Since the lender will obtain an interest in the home once the loan is given, the lender has an economic interest in making sure that the buyer obtains good and valid title to the property. In this sense, the lender is protecting the buyer by making sure that the home being used as security for the loan is not being transferred with a defective title.

Understand that the lender has no legal obligation to represent the interest of the buyer. However, due to the fact that the lender is obtaining security in the home being purchased, the lender has a vested interest in making sure that the title to the home is sound.

APPRAISERS As mentioned in the previous section, a loan is often necessary to allow the buyer to purchase the home. To make sure that the home is worth what the buyer is willing to pay for it, the lender will likely require an *appraisal* of the home. The purpose of the appraisal is to protect the lender so that the amount of money being lent is less than the actual value of the home. This becomes important in the event that the buyer should default and the lender has to enforce its security interest and sell the home to recover its money.

Most states do not require any formal educational or apprenticeship background to qualify as an appraiser. However, there are various designations that an appraiser can earn, with certain designations such as IFA (Independent Fee Appraiser) being rather common, while the MAI (Member, Appraisal Institute) is more prestigious and requires a great deal of study to achieve. In any event, the only criterion an appraiser generally must have is to convince the person he is working for that he is qualified, either through experience or formal education, to make an informed estimate as to the worth of the home.

Even though an appraiser may be paid by the lender, an appraiser does not represent the lender in any capacity and his appraisal figure would, theoretically, be the same whether he was being paid by the lender, the buyer, or the seller. An appraiser's final figure is considered an objective third party opinion regarding the value of a home.

The appraisal of the home becomes especially important with loans guaranteed by the Veterans Administration (VA) or Federal Housing

Administration (FHA). These types of loans are discussed in Chapter 3, on financing.

If the buyer is attempting to procure a VA or FHA loan, and the appraisal is less than the purchase agreement price, the buyer will not be obligated to purchase the home. Also, any earnest money deposit will be returned to the buyer. The purchase agreement should always contain a clause specifying the buyer's rights in this regard if a VA or FHA loan is involved. This type of provision is often referred to as a *VA/FHA escape clause*.

2

The Purchase Agreement

The purchase agreement for buying a home is undoubtedly the most important document in the transaction. It is literally the cornerstone upon which the rest of the purchase is built. The express and implied terms of this agreement constitute a legally binding contract that governs the responsibilities and actions of the buyer and the seller. This chapter will help the reader understand both the necessary and desirable elements used in the agreement to buy a home, and the consequences of each. You may want to refer to the Purchase Agreement in the Appendix as you go through this chapter.

ESSENTIAL ELEMENTS OF THE PURCHASE AGREEMENT

The law requires that certain specific elements be included or contained in any contract, including a contract to buy a home. These include the following: an offer (by the buyer); an acceptance of the offer (by the seller); and *consideration* for the sale.

The word *consideration*, when used in contract law, can be defined as an act or a promise bargained for and transferred in exchange for another act or promise. The element of consideration in a real estate purchase agreement is the purchase price being exchanged for ownership of the home.

Other necessary elements in a real estate purchase agreement include the existence of the subject matter and the legality of the contract. With regard to the existence of the subject matter, there must be a meeting of the minds between the buyer and the seller as to the actual home being sold. For example, if the buyer is referring to the property at 117 Elm Street, while the seller is mistakenly referring to the house at 717 Elm Street, there is no meeting of the minds, and the subject matter of the contract is not the same between the buyer and the seller. Such a contract is potentially unenforceable.

A real estate purchase agreement, like any legally binding contract, must have an element of legality. This means that the contract must be legal and not criminal in nature, and not void as a matter of public policy. Obviously, this is rarely an obstacle when buying or selling a home, except in the case of some type of criminal or civil fraud.

STATUTE OF FRAUDS

In nearly every state there is a law called the *statute of frauds*. This law states, among other things, that a contract for the purchase of a home must be in writing to be enforceable. An oral agreement for the sale of a home cannot be legally enforced. This law is based upon public policy that the transfer of real estate is too important a matter to be left to oral terms, and must be put in writing so that there is no misunderstanding or possible confusion as to what exactly is being sold, for what price, to whom, and so on.

Certain limited exceptions to the statute of frauds do exist, but they should not be relied upon or utilized. If some type of written evidence of the otherwise oral agreement to purchase the home does exist (such as a letter confirming a conversation), the agreement may be enforced.

Also, if the buyer and the seller have relied upon their oral contract by their actions subsequent to the agreement, the statute of frauds can possibly be circumvented. For example, if after entering into an oral contract to purchase a home, the buyer obtained loan approval and the seller obtained marketable title, and then one of the parties decided not to honor the contract, the remaining party might still be able to enforce the otherwise oral contract because of this reliance exception.

These exceptions should not be relied upon, and all contracts for the sale of real estate should be in writing and contain the terms previously mentioned, as well as others that will be discussed shortly.

CASH FOR DEED PURCHASE AGREEMENT

In most cases, a contract to purchase a home will be a *cash for deed* purchase agreement. This means that the buyer needs to obtain the entire purchase price for the home before the seller transfers the deed to the buyer. The first thing that is required to have a valid purchase agreement for a home in a cash for deed situation is an *offer*.

Offer

An *offer* for a home can be defined as a proposal by a potential buyer, intended to create a binding purchase agreement if the offer is accepted by the homeowner. In most situations, an offer is *contingent* in nature. That is, even though the offer may be accepted, certain prerequisites must be met before the buyer is legally required to purchase the home.

Typical contingencies that may be part of an offer include a specified time frame in which the homeowner must respond (accept the offer); or that the offer is contingent upon the buyer selling his existing home; or that the offer is contingent upon the buyer obtaining acceptable financing for the purchase price.

These types of contingencies must be reviewed very carefully by the homeowner. If the offer is accepted, the seller is put in the position of not being able to close on the home unless the contingencies are met.

Acceptance

If the seller agrees unconditionally to the terms of the buyer's offer, an acceptance has been made. If both the offer and the acceptance were in writing, a real estate purchase agreement has been created.

It is important to remember that the homeowner's acceptance of the buyer's offer must not change the terms of the original offer in any way, shape, or form. If the seller agrees to the buyer's offer but changes some of the terms of the offer in his acceptance, an acceptance has not really occurred. Rather, a *counter offer* has been created. The counter offer must then be reviewed by the buyer and either accepted, rejected, or otherwise responded to in a counter-counter offer.

These offers and counter offers can go back and forth several times before one of them is accepted unconditionally and the purchase agreement is finalized. Often, it is the purchase price itself that is being negotiated during this offer/counter offer stage.

Date Every purchase agreement for the sale of a home should contain the date of the agreement. If the offer is made on a certain date, that date should be noted on the agreement. If an acceptance is made on a subsequent date, that date should also be on the agreement.

As discussed in the preceding paragraphs, certain contingencies in the agreement often involve a specific time limit. This makes the date of the agreement critical. It is always good practice to date any signature on a legally binding document, whether it is a real estate purchase agreement or another type of document.

Parties The names of the buyer and the seller should be contained in the agreement. Furthermore, the marital status of the buyer and the seller should also be specifically stated. This is because many states have laws that give spouses an interest in each other's property, including the home being bought or sold, regardless of how the title to the property is actually held.

If the seller or the buyer has an authorized agent who is representing his interests, that agent can in most circumstances sign the purchase agreement for him. Usually, a legally valid agent for a buyer or a seller in a purchase agreement must be in receipt of a *general power of attorney* or court order authorizing him to execute documents for the buying or selling of real estate.

Any such agent should clearly state in the purchase agreement that he is the agent for either the buyer or the homeowner, and not acting on his own behalf. It is always best, however, to have the actual buyer or seller personally sign the agreement.

It is not necessarily fatal to the purchase agreement if one of the parties does not sign. The circumstances surrounding the transactions will determine whether the actual signatures are absolutely required. Often, some type of actionable acquiescence by the non-signing party is sufficient if reasonably relied upon by the other party to the agreement. For example, if the seller is not available to sign the purchase agreement at the time the offer is made, and the buyer needs to know immediately whether the offer will be accepted, the seller can verbally agree to the offer and create a binding contract. Often, the seller formally signs the contract at a later date.

This situation can occur when the seller is out of town when an offer is made.

The question often arises as to whether the signatures to a real estate purchase agreement must be notarized. Unless there is a specific law requiring this in the jurisdiction involved, notarization is not a requirement. A public notary is merely stating that the person who is signing a document is, in fact, that person whom he purports to be. The notarization element to a real estate purchase agreement, or any other type of contract, only creates a legal presumption that the person signing the document is in fact the person named in the agreement.

Earnest Money Deposit Most purchase agreements for a home involve an earnest money deposit. An *earnest money deposit* can be defined as a portion of the purchase price that the buyer forwards to the homeowner, at the time the original offer is made, to show his good faith. If the offer by the buyer is not accepted, the earnest deposit is returned to the buyer. If the offer is accepted, the earnest deposit is held by the homeowner (or his real estate broker) until closing, when it is applied to the purchase price.

The purpose of an earnest deposit is to show the seller that the buyer is indeed serious in wanting to buy the home. It is generally thought that the higher the earnest deposit in comparison with the purchase price, the more serious the buyer. Of course, a large earnest deposit does not necessarily mean that there will not be problems with the sale later in the transaction.

If a purchase agreement has an earnest deposit held by a third party such as a real estate broker, and the buyer fails to follow through with the purchase of the home for no justifiable reason, the earnest deposit can be forwarded to the homeowner as a form of compensation for taking his home off the market during the time that the buyer was apparently proceeding to purchase the home.

Most purchase agreements give the seller the option either to retain the earnest deposit or, in the alternative, to return the earnest deposit to the potential buyer and proceed with whatever other legal remedy or lawsuit the seller chooses. Of course, if any contingency in the purchase agreement is not met due to no fault of the buyer, the earnest deposit is returned to him.

If a dispute arises as to whether the buyer is entitled to a return of the earnest deposit, or whether the homeowner is to keep it as a form of damages, any third party holding the earnest deposit is obligated to hold the money until the dispute is resolved. Sometimes this earnest money deposit will be turned over to and held by the court that has jurisdiction over any lawsuit filed between the parties.

Method of Payment A statement as to how the buyer is going to obtain the purchase money should also be included in the purchase agreement. This is almost without exception the prime contingency in any real estate purchase agreement. The buyer's obligation to purchase the home will be contingent upon his obtaining suitable financing.

Generally, the buyer will have to obtain third party financing from either a bank or a mortgage company. Most lenders require that a purchase agreement be signed by the buyer and the seller before proceeding with the loan process.

The type of financing, including acceptable interest rate and costs of the loan, should be specifically stated in the purchase agreement. If the costs of the loan are higher than the stated rate in the purchase agreement, the buyer has no legal obligation to purchase the home.

When a buyer must obtain financing at a certain interest rate or specific amount prior to being legally obligated to purchase the home, it is incumbent upon the buyer to make all reasonable and good faith efforts to obtain that financing. That is, a contingency in a purchase agreement that the buyer does not reasonably try to meet will not be a legally valid method of canceling the enforceability of the contract. Thus, the agreement should specifically state that the buyer will make a good faith effort to meet all contingencies in the purchase agreement.

The Deed The purchase agreement should provide that, when the buyer does obtain the purchase price as agreed upon, the homeowner must transfer a deed to the buyer at the time of closing. The particular type of deed to be transferred should also be set forth in the agreement. There are several types of deeds, including *warranty deeds, quitclaim deeds, bargain and sale deeds*, and others. Generally, a warranty deed is used for the sale of residential real estate. An in-depth discussion of the different types of deeds and their legal ramifications is included in Chapter 5.

Property Description A description of the home being sold should also be part of the agreement. Generally, both the street address and the *legal description* should be used to avoid any confusion as to the exact property involved.

A legal description is considered a more precise manner of defining the property. In a residential situation, a plat map is often used in which the lot where the home is located has a specific number. In such a case, the legal description could be stated as follows: "Lot 27, Greentree Subdivision, City of Lincoln, County of Douglas, State of Nebraska."

Other types of legal descriptions, where the home is not included in a specific plat map, refer to the general area involved and can be very elaborate or very simple, referring to different *metes and bounds* (geographical reference points) to determine the exact property being sold. The legal description of the home can be obtained from public records at the local courthouse or by a local real estate title company.

Evidence of Title Before the buyer becomes obligated to pay the purchase price, the homeowner must prove *evidence of title*. This means that the homeowner must show (to the satisfaction of the buyer) that he does in fact own the home and is able to transfer ownership to the buyer. Different jurisdictions have different ways of proving evidence of title.

In some jurisdictions, an *attorney's opinion* is used. That is, a real estate attorney reviews the history of the property being sold and then issues a formal written opinion to the buyer stating that, in his professional opinion, the home is legally owned by the seller and can be effectively transferred to the buyer without fear of any potential third party claims.

Another common method of indicating evidence of title is a *title insurance policy*. In this case, an insurance company does an independent investigation and *searches the title*. The company reviews the legal history of the previous ownership of the home and determines to its satisfaction that the seller (and in turn the buyer when the purchase agreement is effected) is the legal owner of the home and capable of an effective transfer of good title. The cost of an attorney's opinion or title insurance is usually paid for by either the buyer or the seller, or sometimes split, depending upon what is agreed upon in the purchase agreement.

Possession The possession date of the home should be stated in the purchase agreement. In most situations, the date of the transfer of title coincides with the date of possession. However, the occupancy of the home sometimes occurs either before or after the deed is transferred. If this is so, the purchase agreement should specifically provide that a separate written document for this early or late occupancy will be executed by the parties at or prior to closing. A more in-depth discussion of early-late occupancy agreements is found in Chapter 5.

Taxes and Utilities Most homes have the ongoing expense of real estate taxes and utilities. The purchase agreement typically provides that these expenses be prorated up to the date of closing. In essence, this means that the buyer assumes liability for these expenses when he becomes owner of the home, while the seller is liable for them prior to the deed being transferred. The costs for these types of continuing expenses are usually credited or debited between the homeowner and the buyer at the time of closing and adjusted accordingly in the final closing statements.

Other Contingencies Generally, any type of contingency that the buyer and seller agree on may be placed in the purchase agreement. Examples include the contingency that the homeowner is not obligated to sell the home until he has purchased another home; or that the agreement, even though already signed, is only enforceable and valid upon review and approval by either the buyer's or the seller's attorney.

Date of Closing The date that the home is to close—when the buyer is to receive the deed in exchange for the purchase price—should be mentioned in the real estate purchase agreement. Often, however, this closing date is stated: "as soon as reasonably possible."

This is not fatal to the agreement or necessarily unwise, as it is often difficult to determine how much time will pass between the date of the purchase agreement and when the actual closing will occur. This is so because often it is impossible to know how much time it will take for the buyer to obtain financing, or to sell his existing home, or any number of other contingencies contained in the purchase agreement.

The agreement should at least contain a *target date* so there is some reference to an approximate closing date to which both the buyer and the seller have agreed.

You should always remember that unless the critical phrase *time is of the essence* is contained in the agreement, any date contained in the real estate purchase agreement, including the closing or possession date, is considered merely a target date. Because of the inherent uncertainties as to how long various elements in the real estate purchase agreement will take to effect, including all contingencies, if a specific date is not met, it does not allow one of the parties to declare the contract null and void. Only if the agreement specifically states that time is of the essence regarding a certain date will missing such a date be considered a legal basis for breaching the contract.

Recording the Purchase Agreement A question that sometimes arises is whether or not the purchase agreement needs to be recorded in a local public office, such as the register of deeds. As will be seen later on, the recording of the agreement may become crucial to other types of purchase agreements for a home. However, when the agreement is a cash for deed type of purchase, the recording of the purchase agreement is not necessary or even desirable.

If the purchase agreement does not eventually result in an actual sale, it would be very difficult for the homeowner to remove the effect that the recording of the agreement would have on the title to the home. As indicated earlier, any buyer will require that the seller prove that he has evidence of title prior to closing. If a recorded purchase agreement between the homeowner and a previous potential buyer is a matter of public record, a *cloud* is placed on the title. It would consequently be very difficult for the homeowner to evidence good title to a subsequent buyer. There is no real legal or practical reason to record a cash for deed purchase agreement in the absence of some unusual circumstance to the contrary.

Personal Property or Fixtures Certain items that most people assume are part of the home may not, in fact, legally be part of the home. For instance, most draperies and curtains do not stay with the home upon sale. The seller is legally justified in taking these items with him after the sale has occurred. The buyer may not realize this. Accordingly, any type of personal property that stays with the home after the sale should be specifically enumerated in the agreement so as to avoid any potential confusion.

As a general rule, any item that is permanently attached to the home is considered a *fixture* and will stay with the home upon sale unless otherwise agreed. The question then is, what constitutes a fixture? This issue has led to many court disputes. Is a full-length mirror bolted to the wall in the entry a fixture? Are the rods that hold up draperies and are attached to the walls of the home fixtures? Is the birdbath in the backyard, buried inches in the ground, a fixture? It would be easy for the homeowner to assume that these items of personal property are not included in the sale, while the buyer may just as easily assume that these same items should remain with the home.

As mentioned, to avoid any such disputes, all such questionable items should be specifically provided for in the purchase agreement so both the buyer and the seller know from the outset exactly what is included in the home. Most real estate brokers will be able to assist the homeowner and the buyer in determining what is typically considered a fixture.

Closing Costs

With any transfer of a home, certain unavoidable costs come into play. Included are the *discount points* that the buyer is sometimes required to pay the lender to obtain the loan. A discount point is one percent of the loan amount. Generally, the lower the rate of the loan, the higher the number of discount points that accompany it.

In regard to the real estate purchase agreement, the cost of any discount points is negotiable between the buyer and the seller. That is, the homeowner may agree to pay all or part of the buyer's points as an incentive to sell the home, if not prohibited from doing so by the lender due to the type of loan being made.

Other types of typical closing costs include a termite inspection, radon inspection, and other types of structural inspections on the home. All will generally need to be made prior to closing. The costs of these inspections are purely negotiable and may be paid for by either the buyer or the homeowner, or split between them. Often, local custom or policy dictates which party pays for what in this regard.

As mentioned earlier, the homeowner must be able to evidence title. There is usually a cost for this, either for an attorney's opinion or for title insurance. It should be stated in the purchase agreement whether the buyer or the seller is liable for the cost. Often the cost is divided equally.

When the deed to the home is transferred at closing, it will usually be recorded in a local public office in the county where the home is located. In most cases, a charge is made for this recording. Local business custom often dictates who pays for these recording costs. The cost of recording the deed (and any other locally required document of transfer) is open to negotiation and should be provided for in the purchase agreement so that the parties clearly understand the costs for which they are responsible.

Pre-Closing Insurance
Typically, there are several weeks or more between the date the purchase agreement is signed and the date of closing. Due to this inherent time gap, some mention should be made in the purchase agreement as to the risk of loss of the home during this time. The homeowner is usually obligated to maintain both liability and casualty insurance on the home until the time of closing.

Many states have enacted the Uniform Vendor and Purchaser Risk Act. This law states that if the closing of the purchase has not occurred, and there is a material destruction to the home, the buyer is not legally obligated to purchase the home and is entitled to the return of any earnest deposit. A statement to this effect should be included in the purchase agreement if the Uniform Vendor and Purchase Risk Act is not law in the particular state where the home is located.

LAND INSTALLMENT SALES CONTRACT

A *land installment sales contract*, also known as a *land contract for deed, installment land contract*, or *land contract*, is a different type of instrument than a cash for deed purchase agreement. In essence, in a land installment sales contract, the buyer makes periodic payments over an extended period of time to the seller rather than paying one lump sum at the time of closing as in the cash for deed purchase agreement.

In effect, the homeowner is acting as the lender. The buyer does not have to obtain a loan since he does not have to pay the entire purchase price at closing. Generally, the transfer of the deed to the home does not occur until the buyer has made all the payments to the seller. During the time that the payments are being made, the seller is deemed to have *legal title* while the buyer is considered to have *equitable title*. This means that both parties have a legal interest in the home during the contract period.

Essential Provisions of a Land Installment Sales Contract

As stated earlier, the statute of frauds requires that all purchase agreements for selling a home be in writing to be enforceable. Land installment sales contracts are included in this statute of frauds requirement.

Generally, the following elements must be contained in the land installment sales contract to make it enforceable: the names of the buyer and the seller, a description of the home, the price being paid, and the method of payment. With regard to method of payment, the contract should state how much money is to be initially paid by the buyer; the amount of monthly, quarterly, or annual payments thereafter; how long the payments are to continue; and what portion of each payment constitutes interest and what portion constitutes principal.

The land installment sales contract should contain a specific provision for when the deed will be transferred. This will usually occur on the date that the last payment has been made from the buyer to the seller. The seller will not often agree to transfer the deed until all the money has been received. However, there are some exceptions to this, and whatever the buyer and the seller agree to in the contract will generally be acceptable with regard to when the deed is to be transferred.

Escrow Agent Some land installment sales contracts will have a third party as an *escrow agent*. Since land installment sales contracts can potentially go on for several years before all the payments have been made, the escrow agent becomes involved to make sure that both parties meet their obligations and that no difficulties arise in transferring the deed. If an escrow agent is used, the land contract will usually be recorded in the appropriate public office, making it a matter of record.

During the life of the contract, the escrow agent will usually hold the deed that has been previously executed by the seller. The deed is executed by the seller and given to the escrow agent at the time the land contract is entered into. Then, once the buyer has made all his payments as provided for in the contract, the deed is forwarded to the buyer. This acts as an assurance to the buyer that he will receive the deed to the home once all the payments are made.

Under this escrow agent arrangement, if some factor arises during the contract period that might have prevented or delayed the deed from being transferred, such as the death or bankruptcy of the seller, the buyer will still obtain the deed to the home from the escrow agent once all payments have been made.

A land installment contract buyer usually takes possession of the home when the land contract is signed, even though he does not yet have the legal title to the property. If the buyer should stop making payments to the seller, but the land contract has been previously recorded, a cloud on the title to the property will exist, which would probably prevent the seller from selling the property to another buyer immediately.

Hence, to assure that the seller has a viable and fairly simple option to remove this cloud, a deed previously executed by the buyer to the seller is signed at the time the land contract is executed. It is held by the escrow agent during the life of the contract. If the buyer stops making the payments under the terms of the contract, the seller notifies the escrow agent of this fact, and the escrow agent forwards this previously executed deed from the buyer to the seller. The seller then records this deed, and by doing so removes the potential cloud on the title to the home.

Whenever an escrow agent is involved in this type of contract, a separate escrow agent agreement must be drawn up specifically giving the escrow agent the authority previously described. The escrow agent is often paid a fee, with the buyer and the seller dividing the cost.

Closing The closing of the land installment sales contract is different than a cash for deed type closing. In a land installment sales contract closing, there are really two closings. The first closing is when the agreement is signed. The second closing is when all payments are made, and the deed is actually transferred from the seller to the buyer. Often several years pass between this initial closing and the final closing. Land installment contract closings are discussed in Chapter 4.

Possession   Possession of the home is almost always given to the buyer during the life of the land installment sales contract. This fact should be specifically contained in the agreement so there is no confusion that the buyer does have the right to possess the home during the contract period.

By maintaining possession of the home, the buyer is providing what is called *actual notice* to any third party that the buyer has equitable title to the home. This becomes important in case the seller tries to sell the home to another person during the time that the buyer is making payments. That is, if a dispute should arise between the first buyer and the second buyer, the paramount issue in deciding who has the greater right to the home will be whether the second buyer had notice of the first buyer.

If the buyer is not occupying the property during the agreement period, the contract should be recorded in the appropriate local public office. Once the agreement is recorded, it provides the rest of the world with what is called *constructive notice* that the buyer has certain rights in the home.

These actual or constructive notice provisions benefit the buyer. They make it difficult for a dishonest seller to sell or transfer the home to someone else during the life of the contract.

Improvements and Upkeep   The land installment sales contract should also contain a provision stating whether the buyer has the right to make improvements on the home during the term of the contract. If the buyer wants to make an addition to the home or build on the property, this anticipated improvement should be specifically allowed by the seller and stated as such in the agreement. If the seller wants to prohibit any such improvements during the term of the contract, this also should be provided for in the contract.

Often included in a land installment sales contract is a statement that it is the buyer's responsibility to maintain the home during the agreement period. This provision not only refers to basic structural maintenance, but also makes it the buyer's responsibility to pay all real estate taxes, insurance, and utilities on the home. It is not uncommon for the seller to require that the buyer provide evidence that these types of payments are being made so as not to cause the home to fall into disrepair, tax foreclosure, and the like during the contract period.

OPTION TO PURCHASE   Sometimes a potential buyer will not, for one reason or another, be ready to enter into a purchase agreement for a home. However, he may want to control that home in the sense that he would like to have the first right to purchase the property. In this regard, an *option to purchase* comes into play. (There is an example of an Option to Purchase in the Appendix.)

An option to purchase can be defined as a real estate contract between the homeowner and a potential buyer in which the potential buyer pays for the right to possibly purchase the home within a specified time in the future. His future right to purchase the home necessarily disallows anyone else from buying the home during the option period without the option holder's consent.

Legal Requirements of an Option to Purchase

To have an option to purchase a home that is legally enforceable, the option must be paid for by the potential buyer. That is, the seller cannot gratuitously give an option to another as this lacks the necessary element of consideration, as discussed earlier. For the buyer to enforce an option to purchase, some consideration (usually money) must be given. If the option is not paid for, the seller will have no obligation to allow the potential buyer the first right to purchase the home and may sell the home to another buyer without any legal prohibitions.

The manner in which the buyer exercises his option—the notice from the potential buyer to the seller that the potential buyer now wants to purchase the home—should be specifically set forth in the option agreement. Generally, the notice requires that the buyer indicate to the seller in writing within a certain period of time that he now desires to purchase the home.

It is always best, and in some states a requirement, to have the specific terms of sale contained in the option agreement. This is so that if and when the option is exercised, a valid purchase agreement and all its necessary terms will exist immediately. Without the terms of the sale being agreed upon in the option itself, the exercise of the option only opens up the avenues of negotiation. An option, in that case, is not a true option to purchase but merely an option to make an offer, which may or may not be accepted by the seller.

BREACH OF THE PURCHASE AGREEMENT: REMEDIES TO THE BUYER AND SELLER

Home purchase agreements are often the basis of legal disputes. The stakes (and the emotions) can be high, as often the terms of the purchase agreement are not completely understood by either the buyer or the seller. A dispute will usually arise when one of the parties has *breached the contract*. A breach of contract occurs when either the buyer or the seller has not met his obligation under the terms of the contract. When this happens, the non-breaching party has several types of legal recourse available.

Cash for Deed Purchase Agreement

In a cash for deed purchase agreement, if the buyer does not meet his obligation to purchase the home, the homeowner will often retain the earnest deposit as compensation. The homeowner will take the earnest deposit money as a form of *liquidated damages*, cut his losses, move on, and try to find another buyer. Liquidated damages is a predetermined sum that the parties to a contract have agreed will be the amount that the non-breaching party is entitled to in the event of a breach of contract.

Generally, the purchase agreement states that the seller may either keep the earnest deposit or proceed with formal legal action. The cost of litigation and the chance of losing the lawsuit, however, usually lead the seller to decide to retain the earnest deposit and place the home back on the market.

If the seller wishes to hold the buyer liable for damages (as opposed to keeping the earnest deposit), he must prove that he lost money or was otherwise harmed due to the buyer's breach of the contract. In determining his losses, the seller does have the duty to *mitigate his damages*. This means that he must attempt to re-sell the home as soon as reasonably possible, for as high a price as possible.

If, in fact, the homeowner sells the property for the same or a higher price immediately after the breach by the first buyer, he probably does not have damages that would make a lawsuit worthwhile. But if the home does not resell immediately, or sells at a much lower price than the first buyer was willing to pay, the buyer may be legally responsible for the homeowner's resulting losses.

If the homeowner does not sell the home as required by the purchase agreement, he may be in breach of the contract. In such a case, the buyer may be able to require *specific performance.* That is, the buyer can obtain a court order that will require the homeowner specifically to perform his part of the purchase agreement—transfer the home to the buyer. Of course, the buyer must also be able to pay the seller the agreed upon purchase price and abide by the other terms of the purchase agreement.

Often, however, the buyer will be satisfied to recover his earnest deposit and resume his search for a home rather than proceed with a protracted court case enforcing the homeowner to transfer the home in question. However, since each particular parcel of real estate is considered unique, the law will allow the buyer to pursue this specific performance remedy if so desired.

Keep in mind that if any breach of a real estate purchase agreement occurs, the non-breaching party has an inherent duty to keep his losses to a minimum. As already mentioned, this is called a duty to mitigate. Once this obligation is met, however, all damages that either the buyer or the seller can prove were a result of the other's breach are potentially recoverable in court.

Land Installment Sales Contract   With regard to the breach of a land installment sales contract, if the buyer, during the course of the agreement, should stop making the required payments, or does not pay the inherent upkeep on the home such as taxes and insurance, the buyer is generally considered to have breached the contract. At that time, the seller's obligation to transfer the deed to the buyer ends, and he may (with some exceptions as noted below) retain all or part of the periodic payments previously made by the buyer. Of course, the seller must pursue an eviction and/or a foreclosure action to remove the buyer from the home if the buyer continues his occupancy.

Depending upon the length of time involved in the contract and the number of payments missed by the buyer, as compared with the total amount already paid at the time of default, the buyer may have certain equitable rights to the home despite his breach of the contract. This is true even though the buyer does not pay the entire purchase price.

For instance, assume that a land contract required the buyer to pay monthly payments of $500 for twenty years. The buyer faithfully made all the payments for nineteen years and ten months and then missed the final two payments. It is highly unlikely that any court would turn the property back over to the seller and remove the buyer from the home. Most courts would likely award a money judgment in favor of the seller against the buyer for the remaining balance owed. The remedy available to the seller, then, will depend primarily on the particular facts involved, including the extent of the breach, the length of the contract, and the amount of previous payments made by the buyer. The rights of the buyer and the seller vary greatly from state to state and will often turn on the facts of the breach and applicable local laws.

OTHER RELATED ASPECTS OF THE PURCHASE AGREEMENT

It is very seldom that a buyer and a seller sit down to draft a real estate purchase agreement from scratch. Most real estate purchase agreements are provided as a set form, with the specifics to the sale left blank to be completed by the parties. These forms are usually available through local legal stationery stores or are provided by a real estate broker.

Form Agreements

Form agreements can be helpful, but they should not be blindly relied upon to reflect what is required between the buyer and the seller in a particular transaction. Often the sale will have enough unique contingencies or provisions to make a form agreement virtually worthless.

It should also be noted that the courts will usually interpret any ambiguities in a form agreement in the favor of the party who did not provide the form agreement. This is usually the buyer when a real estate broker is involved, since the broker represents the homeowner. It is the seller who would in all likelihood have this interpretation assumption held against him with regard to form agreements provided by his broker.

Even so, most form real estate purchase agreements are not confusing in nature, as they are drafted specifically by local real estate attorneys and are designed to be used in most standard home sales. However, this interpretation aspect should be kept in mind when using any type of form agreement.

Addendums

An *addendum* is either a clarification or an addition to an existing contract. They are often used in real estate purchase agreements to change original terms. Or, if there is some confusion with regard to a term in the initial agreement that is not discovered until after the buyer and the seller have signed, an addendum can be used to clarify this otherwise confusing aspect of the original agreement. Addendums should always be signed by the parties to the original agreement and dated to reflect the date of the addendum (change or clarification) as compared with the original agreement.

General Recommendations One final note with regard to real estate purchase agreements. They are legally binding contracts that can either effectuate a simple purchase of a home or be the focal point of a protracted legal dispute. Never take any term in a real estate purchase agreement for granted, and never execute a real estate purchase agreement without understanding all its terms and phrases. Real estate brokers involved in the sale cannot be held accountable for giving misguided advice with regard to the legal effect of the agreement.

If in doubt, always consult with an attorney before executing the agreement, or include in the agreement a clause stating that any obligations the party may have after signing the agreement are specifically contingent upon the agreement being approved by your attorney within a certain period of time. This creates a legal method of terminating the agreement if the attorney reviewing it so advises.

3

Financing the Purchase of the Home

Few buyers have enough available cash to purchase a home without some type of lending assistance. Much then depends upon how much the buyer will be able to borrow and the amount of interest to be paid on the loan. More than anything else, these factors determine how much home a buyer is able to afford.

As stated in Chapter 2, the most common contingency in real estate purchase agreements is the ability of the buyer to obtain a loan. From the seller's perspective, prevailing interest rates for home loans have a direct effect on how many potential buyers are able to afford to purchase the home. As a general rule, low interest rates increase the likelihood that the homeowner will be able to sell his home quickly.

Institutional lenders will always be willing to loan money to qualified buyers for the purchase of a home, provided that the home is worth enough to protect the lender in case the buyer defaults. Of course, the lender always conducts a thorough credit check on the buyer to assure that the buyer will, in all likelihood, be able to repay the loan.

TYPES OF FINANCING

Cash Sales

As already mentioned, few potential buyers have enough money on hand to purchase a home without the assistance of a lender. Or, possibly, the purchaser does not wish to pay cash so as to take advantage of any tax incentives, such as the deduction of interest on mortgage payments. However, a small portion of home buyers are able and willing to pay cash. These buyers are able to proceed through the sale without a loan approval process that an institutional lender requires. Furthermore, the cash buyer will not have the title to his home subject to a mortgage or other type of security device, but will own the home *free and clear*.

It is usually to the seller's advantage to deal with the cash buyer. Any delay in the buyer obtaining the necessary loan to purchase the home is no longer involved, and, consequently, the home may be sold much more quickly and efficiently, always without the chance that any contingencies in the purchase agreement will not be met.

Of course, the reverse can also be true. That is, if the homeowner is attempting to sell his existing home and at the same time purchase another home, a cash buyer may want to close and take possession immediately. That could potentially leave the seller in a quandary about where to reside until he has located a new residence.

A disadvantage to the cash buyer is that he has no lender guarding his interests in the transaction. Usually, a lender will make sure that the deed to the home is valid, that the title is in acceptable condition, and that the property is worth at least the amount of the loan. Without a lender or some other type of professional representation involved, a cash buyer is totally on his own in this regard and must take all precautions to see that his interests in the purchase are protected.

Mortgages   Much more common than the cash sale is the situation in which the buyer must obtain a loan so he can buy the home. The lender, in exchange for lending the money to the buyer, takes a *security interest* in the home being purchased. A security interest in a home is a legal, enforceable interest for a specific amount (the balance of the loan). The buyer will own the home, subject to the lender's security interest. As long as the buyer makes the required payments to the lender, everything is fine. But if a payment is missed, or some other breach with the lender occurs, the lender may commence with formal legal proceedings (foreclosure) to have the property eventually forcibly transferred from the homeowner to the lender. Foreclosure is discussed in Chapter 5.

Historically, the most common device used to declare and enforce the lender's security interest in the home is called a mortgage. In a mortgage situation, the buyer is lent the money to purchase the home. The buyer is referred to as the *mortgagor*. The company or individual lending the money to the buyer is called the *mortgagee*. The document reflecting the security interest of the lender in the home is the *mortgage*. (There is an example of a Mortgage in the Appendix.)

Once the mortgage is executed by the homeowner, it is recorded in the appropriate public office so as to provide notice to any third party that the mortgage does exist and that, even though the homeowner has the title to the property in his name, it is subject to the lender's security interest.

In general, for an instrument to be effective as a mortgage, the instrument needs to contain the following information: the names of the mortgagee and mortgagor; a description of the property being used as security; reference to a promissory note indicating that the mortgage is given as security for debt; and the specific terms of repaying the debt, if they are not otherwise mentioned in the promissory note. Remember, the promissory note is written evidence of the debt, while the mortgage acts as security for the note.

The mortgage must be signed by the buyer to have a legally binding effect. It must also be executed according to the laws of the state in which the property is located. As stated, the mortgage is then recorded by the lender to provide public notice of the existence of the security interest.

Keep in mind that without specific language to the contrary, the lender does not have a right to possess the home, except upon the homeowner's default. Further, the mortgage agreement always provides that the homeowner is required to keep the home properly insured, naming the lender as co-insured, at least up to the amount still owed on the mortgage. This protects the lender should the home being used as the security be destroyed.

Even though the home is subject to a mortgage, it is the homeowner who remains responsible for the taxes or any other type of special assessments that may be levied or charged to the home during the life of the mortgage.

Some mortgages contain *estoppel certificates*. Estoppel certificates are statements contained in the mortgage where the homeowner indicates that, should he be in default, he will be prohibited from raising any legal defense if the lender attempts to foreclose. In most areas, estoppel certificates have been declared invalid since they waive defenses that homeowners would otherwise be legally entitled to according to applicable state law.

Mortgages can last for different lengths of time. A thirty-year mortgage is most common, although fifteen-year mortgages have become more and more popular.

Once the mortgage and promissory note have been paid in full, the lender files, as a matter of public record, a satisfaction or release document that the mortgage has been paid in full and no longer constitutes a security interest on the property. The homeowner then owns the property free and clear, unless other security interests are in place.

The desired effect of the mortgage during the life of the loan is to keep the homeowner from defaulting on payments and to provide the lender with adequate security for the loan. If the loan payments are not made, the lender may declare the loan to be in default and proceed with a foreclosure lawsuit.

A mortgage on a home usually prevents the homeowner from selling the home without first paying off the mortgage in full. An exception to this rule does exist with regard to assumable loans, as discussed later in this chapter.

Deed of Trust The two party mortgagee-mortgagor situation has been the typical method of obtaining security in real estate. More recently, however, the *deed of trust* has become more popular with lenders as a different method of obtaining security for the home loan. (There is an example of a Deed of Trust in the Appendix.)

In a deed of trust, the deed to the home is transferred from the seller to the buyer. Immediately thereafter, the buyer transfers a deed of trust to a third party, called a *trustee*. Pursuant to the terms of this deed of trust, the trustee is required to hold the deed in trust until all the money is repaid from the buyer to the lender. The lender is called the *beneficiary*, while the buyer (borrower) is called the *trustor*.

In a deed of trust situation, the trustee holds the title to the home for the benefit of both the buyer and the lender, while retaining a *power of sale* over the secured home. When the debt secured by the deed of trust is paid in full, the trustee is obligated to convey the deed of trust back to the buyer, thus negating the lender's security interest.

The trustee has an obligation to both the buyer and the lender. The effect of using a deed of trust instead of a mortgage is as follows: if the homeowner stops making his scheduled monthly payments or otherwise falls into default under some other provision of the loan, the lender will not have to proceed with a mortgage foreclosure action to obtain the deed to the home. As is more specifically discussed in Chapter 5, a deed of trust arrangement allows the lender to proceed quickly and efficiently in enforcing its security interest in the home, should the buyer be in default. A mortgage foreclosure lawsuit, on the other hand, could take several months or even years to complete.

Since a trustee does not require court intervention to enforce the lender's security interest, the lender has much more leverage over a potential defaulting homeowner. The procedure governing deed of trust sales is a matter of local law, and specific notification provisions to the homeowner must be complied with prior to the home being sold to enforce the lender's security interest.

It should be realized that both a mortgage and a deed of trust, by their terms, establish a security interest in real estate in favor of the lender. Neither one of them has a distinct advantage over the other with regard to obtaining this security. However, the difference exists when lenders proceed with enforcing their security interest, with the deed of trust being the more efficient and less costly of the two.

In many areas, buyers who enter into a deed of trust rather than a mortgage are required to sign at closing an *acknowledgment of power of sale*. Since the enforcement provisions of a deed of trust are so radically different (and so much quicker to effectuate) than a mortgage, legislatures wanted to make sure that the buyer was acutely aware of the difference. Typically, this acknowledgment will include the following:

> The trustor (borrower) hereby acknowledges that he has read the trust deed and understands that the trust deed is not a mortgage, and that the power of sale provided for in the trust deed contains substantially different rights and obligations to the trustor (borrower) than does a mortgage in the event of default.

Seller Financing Sometimes a buyer, for various reasons, including bad credit history or lack of credit history, will simply not be able to obtain a large enough loan to allow him to purchase the desired home. Or possibly the buyer desires to assume the existing loan on the home, but will not have enough money otherwise available to pay the homeowner the purchase price above and beyond the loan balance. If this is the situation, a homeowner will sometimes agree to *carry back a second mortgage* to allow the purchase to occur. This is also known as a *purchase money mortgage*.

In a purchase money mortgage, the seller transfers the deed of ownership to the buyer, and the buyer will then continue or commence making payments on the first loan. But the buyer will also have to make monthly payments to the second mortgage holder or deed of trust beneficiary. This second mortgage holder or deed of trust beneficiary would be the seller. This often allows the buyer to purchase the home with no down payment.

Of course, should the buyer default on his payments to the seller who is holding the second mortgage or deed of trust, the homeowner must foreclose, knowing that any interest he takes in the property is subject to that first loan. As can be seen, there exists an inherent risk in a purchase money mortgage. A homeowner should take precautions before providing this type of financing to a potential buyer.

Sometimes a purchase money mortgage will contain a *balloon payment*. That is, the buyer will only be paying the owner of the home a minimal monthly payment for several years. Then, after a certain period of time, a payment for the entire balance will be owed. This is called a balloon payment and generally amounts to whatever amount of money the seller has loaned the buyer pursuant to the second mortgage or deed of trust.

A purchase money mortgage is merely another method to assist the buyer in obtaining the necessary funds to purchase the home. Purchase money mortgages often come into play when a homeowner is not otherwise able to locate a buyer who can purchase the home by other, more traditional methods of financing.

Land Installment Sales Contract

As discussed in Chapter 2, a land installment sales contract is a device in which the seller is in effect financing the entire purchase price. Since the seller is receiving periodic payments from the buyer during the term of the purchase agreement, and not receiving the entire purchase price at the time of closing, the seller acts as the lender for the purchase during the life of the contract.

Many buyers who would not otherwise be able to purchase a home by conventional lending methods can purchase a home through the use of a land installment sales contract. If a lender does not agree to lend the necessary funds to a particular buyer, and a homeowner is not able to find a cash buyer or a buyer able to qualify for a loan, the homeowner may agree to sell his home on a land installment sales contract. A seller who is offering his home for sale on these types of terms will be broadening the potential market of buyers available to purchase the home.

Please keep in mind that a homeowner who does sell his home using a land installment sales contract does run a higher risk of potential default by the buyer. Since this type of buyer is often not a good credit risk in the eyes of conventional lenders, it is somewhat more likely that he will default on the terms of the contract than would other types of buyers. Also, if the seller immediately requires the entire purchase price of his existing home so as to allow him to buy another home, he should never enter into a land installment sales contract due to its protracted payment feature.

The buyer is also somewhat at risk in a land installment sales contract. If the buyer should make all the payments required, and the seller then refuses to transfer the deed to the home, the buyer has little choice but to proceed with some type of formal legal action to require the seller to transfer the deed. This could prove costly to the buyer and substantially delay his complete legal ownership of the home.

If the seller should die, declare bankruptcy, or simply disappear during the life of the land installment sales contract, the buyer's ownership rights to the home can be severely complicated. Of course, these types of problems could be avoided with the use of an escrow agent, as discussed in Chapter 2.

TYPES OF LOANS AND FINANCING TERMINOLOGY

Assumable Loans and Due on Sale Clauses

An *assumable loan* is a loan that can be legally assumed or stepped into by a new buyer. If a homeowner has a loan in his name for a desirable interest rate, and the buyer wishes to take the seller's place in paying on the existing loan, by stepping into the seller's shoes, the buyer may be able to assume the loan and continue with the same mortgage obligation and payment. Any mortgage loan that does not contain a certain *due on sale clause* can be assumed.

However, most mortgage loans have a due on sale clause. This means that if the home is ever sold, the entire remaining balance of the loan must be paid. This, of course, requires the buyer to obtain a new loan for the purchase rather than assuming the seller's mortgage loan.

Most loans guaranteed by the Veterans Administration (VA) or Federal Housing Administration (FHA) are assumable. Only assumable home loans at attractive interest rates are desirable. Of course, what is and what is not an attractive interest rate depends upon the prevailing economic conditions at the time of the sale.

Part of the process of assuming a loan, however, is that the buyer must come up with the difference between the sale price and the amount of the existing loan. For instance, if a $50,000 assumable loan exists on a home that is sold for $70,000, the buyer must obtain $20,000 payable to the seller to assume the loan. The only exception to this would be if the seller decides to carry back a second mortgage (purchase money mortgage), which would allow the buyer to assume the first mortgage while also creating a second mortgage on the home.

One very important point to remember is that unless the seller obtains a *release of liability* from the mortgage company on the loan that is being assumed, and the buyer defaults on the loan, the buyer and the seller are *both* obligated to pay off the mortgage in full. That is, without a release of liability releasing the seller, the lender will hold the seller fully responsible to make the loan payments if the buyer should default. Without this release of liability, the seller remains obligated on the assumed loan.

Consequently, most homeowners try to obtain a release of liability from the lender before allowing a buyer to assume the loan. Of course, the lender will only release the seller from his existing liability if the lender is satisfied that the buyer is as good a credit risk as the seller.

If the seller does not require a release of liability, the buyer will not have to pass any type of credit check with the lender to assume the loan. This obviously makes it easier to sell the home but keeps the seller at risk during the balance of the loan payment period.

Veterans Administration Loan The Veterans Administration (VA) loan was created to allow veterans to finance the purchase of reasonably priced homes with little or no down payment. The loan is available to veterans and certain widows and widowers of veterans who have not remarried.

The VA loan is limited to owner-occupied residential dwellings, or dwellings making up one to four family units. As mentioned, usually no down payment is required, and the loan may not exceed the reasonable value of the home. Generally, the Veterans Administration sets a limit on the amount of money that can be borrowed. This amount changes periodically. Local real estate brokers or the local Veterans Administration office can provide the specific amount currently available for VA home loans.

Federal Housing Administration Loan Federal Housing Administration (FHA) loans are types of loans made by conventional lenders but guaranteed by the FHA. Potential buyers of homes under FHA-insured mortgages do not have to be veterans, but they do have to meet certain minimum requirements. The Secretary of Housing and Urban Development usually sets a maximum rate of interest that cannot be exceeded on FHA-insured loans.

However, a charge is made to the borrower as the premium for this FHA insurance. This insurance is put in place to protect the lender from any loss that may occur from the buyer defaulting on the loan.

The home purchased with an FHA-insured loan must be appraised by an FHA appraiser prior to the loan being made, at cost to the buyer. FHA loans can be insured up to a thirty-year mortgage period. Also, certain specific regulations and requirements must be met prior to the FHA loan guarantee being put into place. Most real estate brokers can provide specific advice as to the requirements involved in obtaining an FHA-insured loan. FHA-insured loans are assumable, which lend to their desirability if the loan is at an attractive interest rate.

Farmers Home Administration Loans A Farmers Home Administration (FmHA) loan is very similar to the aforementioned Federal Housing Administration loan. However, it applies only to residential properties located in rural or other non-urban communities. Again, these loans are generally assumable and otherwise entail the same procedural elements as FHA-insured loans.

Conventional Loan   A loan made by a conventional lender has no VA or FHA type of insured protection. Consequently, the lender is at a somewhat higher risk. However, mortgage insurance can be purchased from the private sector through such types of agencies as the Mortgage Guarantee Insurance Corporation (MGIC).

Since the lender is taking a higher risk because the loan is not guaranteed by a state or federal agency, the risk may be reflected in both a higher interest rate and a larger required down payment. There are various types of conventional loans that are available, and their terms vary depending upon whether they are fixed rate, adjustable rate, or variable rate in nature.

With some limited exceptions, conventional loans are not assumable. That is, they contain a due on sale clause requiring the homeowner to pay off the loan when the house is sold, thus eliminating the possibility of an assumption.

Escrow Account   Whenever a lender agrees to make a home loan to a buyer, it requires money to be placed in a separate account at the time of closing. This is called an *escrow account*. The money in this account is used by the lender to pay the real estate taxes and insurance on the home during the mortgage period. The homeowner continually replenishes this escrow account through his monthly mortgage payment. The lender typically tries to maintain several months' worth of taxes and insurance in the escrow account so a cash cushion is perpetually in place, in the event the borrower ceases to make his mortgage payments.

Be aware that federal law limits the amount of money that can be held in escrow. The current rule provides that at least once a year the balance of the escrow account must be less than one-sixth of the estimated total annual payments made from the account.

For instance, if the annual taxes and insurance on the home total $4,000, the escrow account balance must drop to $667 or less at some time during the year. This keeps lenders from maintaining unnecessarily large escrow balances.

Fixed Rate Loans   The most popular type of mortgage loan is the *fixed rate loan*. This type of mortgage has a specific set rate of interest that the borrower must pay during the life of the loan. The interest rate on the loan stays the same, no matter what other interest rates and prevailing economic conditions may do. With a fixed rate mortgage, the interest rate does not change over the life of the loan. As a consequence, the monthly payment of principal and interest does not vary in total amount, although more interest than principal will be paid in the early years of the loan, due to the manner in which home loans are amortized.

Adjustable or Variable Rate Loans   Another type of loan is called the adjustable rate mortgage (ARM). With an adjustable rate mortgage, the interest rate and monthly payment can change; it can either go up or down, depending upon economic conditions or the terms of the mortgage.

Generally, the initial interest rate on an adjustable rate mortgage is lower than that of a fixed rate mortgage. But if interest rates later rise, the mortgage payment increases. Hence, a homeowner can initially pay less on a monthly basis for the loan, but at the same time he will be at risk if interest rates rise.

Some adjustable rate loans are tied to a specific economic index, such as the Treasury Bill Index of the federal government. If this index changes, depending upon prevailing economic conditions, the interest rate on the loan correspondingly increases or decreases. These types of adjustable rate mortgages are also called variable rate mortgages, since the amount of interest and the interest rate itself vary during the life of the mortgage.

Often, the amount of increase will be limited, or *capped*. That is, there may be a maximum amount that the interest rate can increase, regardless of how much the interest rate could potentially increase if the cap was not in place.

Other types of adjustable rate mortgages have specific predetermined schedules that are followed during the life of the loan. For instance, the initial rate of interest may be 7 percent for twelve months, and then escalate to 8 percent for the next twenty-four months, and then remain at 9½ percent for the balance of the mortgage. The initial rate is usually lower than what is available for fixed rate loans, but may end up higher as the loan period continues. Obviously, if the buyer is only planning to stay in the home for a short period of time, an adjustable rate mortgage of this type would be beneficial.

Interest Rates At the time the loan is applied for, buyers will usually have the opportunity to *lock in* an interest rate. By agreeing to lock in a certain interest rate, the lender commits to provide the buyer with this rate for a specific period of time, called the *commitment period*. If the loan is not approved and the closing has not occurred by the end of the commitment period, the interest rate is subject to being increased and is no longer guaranteed by the lender.

Sometimes the buyer will choose to *float* the interest rate. This means that the lender will only be obligated to provide the buyer with whatever interest rate the lender is offering at the time of closing.

Discount Points and Par Rate A buyer is expected to pay certain up-front costs for the loan, such as *discount points*, and credit application and loan origination fees. Recall that a discount point is one percent of the loan amount. Since points are a function of interest rates, the lower the interest rate, the higher the number of points. The interest rate available without any payment of points is termed the *par rate*. Buyers not willing to procure a lower interest rate by paying points may opt for the par rate.

For example, a buyer may be able to obtain a 9 percent loan for no points (par rate) but can also obtain an 8½ percent loan by paying one point. Assuming the loan amount is $50,000, the buyer will need to decide if he can afford to pay an additional $500 at the time of closing in exchange for a somewhat lower monthly payment for the balance of the loan due to the lower interest rate being charged.

Except for VA loans, it can be agreed to in the purchase agreement that the seller pays some, all, or none of the discount points of the buyer's loan. Sellers are legally required to pay any and all of the buyer's discount points if the buyer is obtaining a VA loan.

Caps and Negative Amortization

Adjustable rate mortgages are the type of loan in which the interest rates and payments are not fixed but adjusted over the life of the loan to stay roughly comparable with prevailing market rates. As stated earlier, caps are sometimes involved with adjustable rate mortgages.

Interest rate caps limit how much the interest rate can increase or decrease. Payment caps, however, limit how much the monthly payment can change from one adjustment period to the next. If the buyer's adjustable rate mortgage has a payment cap, *negative amortization* may result.

Negative amortization means that the mortgage balance is increasing despite the fact that the monthly mortgage payment is being applied to the mortgage balance. This occurs whenever the monthly mortgage payment is not large enough to pay all the interest due on the loan. Because payment caps limit only the amount of payment increases, and not interest rate increases, the monthly payment obligation may not cover all the interest due on the loan.

The upshot of this is that the interest shortage in the monthly mortgage payment is automatically added to the debt, and interest may be charged on that amount. Therefore, the buyer may owe the lender more later in the loan term than was owed at the beginning.

Blanket Loans or Mortgages

There are other types of mortgages besides fixed rate and adjustable rate mortgages. One type is the *blanket mortgage*. This is a mortgage loan in which the mortgage includes more than one piece of real estate. In this situation, the lender is not required to release any one portion of the real estate from the mortgage until the balance owed on all the property has been paid. Until such time as it is totally paid, the lender is entitled to retain a security interest on all the real estate during the life of the mortgage.

Package Mortgage Loan

A *package mortgage* loan is the type of loan that involves personal property as well as real estate. Personal property is any type of tangible property that is not real estate. In a package mortgage, a loan is made for the purchase of both real estate and personal property, and both the real estate and personal property are used as security until the loan debt is paid in full.

These loans are somewhat rare, but they do allow the buyer to finance personal property at generally a lower rate of interest than would be charged at retail establishments. However, the buyer is, in effect, extending the time of repayment several years, and, due to the more rapid depreciation of personal property, he may be paying for it well beyond its useful life.

Open End Mortgage An *open end mortgage* can be defined as a mortgage in which the buyer is allowed additional funds from the lender, usually up to the original amount borrowed, under the same security agreement (mortgage) and usually at the original interest rate. Thus, an open end mortgage allows the buyer a set line of credit up to the amount of the security. To be termed an effective open end mortgage, it is often required that the mortgage document include a reference to *future advancements*.

Construction Mortgage A *construction mortgage* provides that a lender periodically advances money to a buyer as construction needs require. This type of loan is usually used by professional builders or new home buyers. The security for the money periodically advanced is the home being built. Thus, the security of the lender escalates in value as the money lent to the buyer increases.

Rollover Mortgage A *rollover mortgage* is a type of loan that is mandatorily renegotiated on a periodic basis. Various federal and state regulations specifically provide how often a rollover mortgage can be renegotiated. Rollover mortgages provide an effective means for the lender to maintain the interest rate on the loan in accordance with current money market conditions.

Co-Signing If a buyer is having difficulty obtaining a loan, sometimes the lender will suggest having a third party guarantee the loan. That is, even though the borrower is giving the lender a security interest (either mortgage or deed of trust) in the home being purchased, the lender additionally requires a co-signer.

Thus, if the borrower defaults, not only can the lender foreclose on the home, but it can also proceed against the buyer and the co-signer for any remaining money owed not received from the foreclosure action. Usually the lender can legally pursue either or both the buyer or the co-signer.

4

The Closing

The closing of a sale on a home is the time when the buyer and the seller transfer their respective interests: the purchase price is exchanged for the deed. The actual closing date of the real estate sale can be likened to the tip of an iceberg, with the bulk of work and preparation occurring days and weeks prior to the date of the actual transfer of ownership.

INDIVIDUALS INVOLVED IN THE CLOSING

Beyond the seller and the buyer, often many more individuals and entities are involved in bringing the transaction to closing. An appreciation of the roles these individuals play will give the seller and the buyer a better understanding of what to expect at closing.

Real Estate Brokers

In most cases, any real estate brokers involved in a sale of a home will be the prime source of professional assistance in assuring that the purchase closes smoothly and in a timely manner. Most sellers rely heavily on their brokers to guide them in meeting the contingencies in the purchase agreement and subsequently closing the transaction.

After the purchase agreement has been executed, the broker will assist the seller and answer any questions the seller may have to facilitate the sale to closing. However, at the actual time and date of closing, a *settlement clerk* or *closing secretary* usually handles the execution of the closing documents and related responsibilities of the seller.

It is common for the seller not to be present at closing, but rather to execute the necessary documents immediately prior to closing. If the broker's real estate company does not have an assigned settlement clerk, the broker may handle the closing on behalf of the seller.

In most circumstances, the buyer is not legally represented in any fashion by real estate brokers throughout the transaction. The only exception to this would be if the buyer has a specific agency agreement with a broker, providing that the broker is to represent his interests.

It is common, however, for the broker to do whatever he can in working with the seller and the buyer to make sure the closing occurs. After all, it is not until the actual day of closing that the broker receives his commission. This economic factor usually provides enough incentive for the broker to assist (but not legally represent) the buyer.

Attorneys Because the purchase of a home is a major transaction, attorneys are often retained to protect the parties' interests. An attorney who represents the seller in a real estate sale provides representation beyond that provided by the real estate broker.

The seller's attorney will make sure that the seller receives all that is due him under the terms of the purchase agreement. If no problems exist with the seller's title to the home, the role of the seller's attorney's is fairly straightforward: do everything possible to make sure that the seller receives the sale price from the buyer in exchange for the deed.

The role of the seller's attorney becomes somewhat more complicated, however, if problems with the title occur prior to closing. These title problems usually present themselves as an encumbrance or a cloud on the title that will need to be removed before the buyer is obligated to close. Usually these encumbrances stem from some type of prior legal action against the seller. In these situations, the attorney for the seller provides professional assistance in removing the encumbrances so that the sale can close.

An attorney representing the buyer must be sure that the buyer receives everything that is due him under the terms of the purchase agreement. The buyer's attorney must: (1) allow the buyer to receive good and valid title to the home; (2) make sure that the home is in the physical condition represented in the purchase agreement; (3) make sure that the home has no other legal defects not otherwise agreed to in the purchase agreement.

For example, if a survey done on behalf of the buyer indicates that the home is not actually the property represented in the purchase agreement, the buyer's attorney must inform the buyer of this fact and present the buyer with various options. These options could include modifying the price of the purchase, canceling the purchase agreement and negating the sale, or allowing the seller to cure the defect prior to closing.

Generally, an attorney representing the buyer spends the bulk of his time reviewing the various documents provided by the title insurance company and surveyor so that the buyer will receive, through the deed, title to the home without any defects or future potential problems. Third parties with any type of legal interest in the home are not bound by the terms of the purchase agreement between the seller and the buyer. Thus, if any third parties have a legal interest in the home, the buyer's attorney must either void that interest or, in the alternative, inform the seller of the problem and allow the seller a reasonable time to correct the problem before closing.

On occasion, the buyer and the seller will approach an attorney and ask that attorney to make sure that all the legal requirements of the purchase are met. The attorney should initially clarify his role by indicating that he is obligated to represent only one party in a real estate sale. Since the buyer and the seller have different interests and requirements, it is impossible for an attorney to represent effectively both the buyer and the seller.

Title Insurance Companies In a typical real estate purchase agreement, the seller must provide good and valid title to the buyer before the buyer is obligated to provide the purchase price. What this usually means is that title insurance must be procured by the seller.

In essence, a title insurance policy insures that if any defects in the title later arise to the detriment of the buyer, the title insurance company will reimburse the buyer for any damage caused by these defects. If a loan is required to purchase the home, the lender will almost always require that title insurance be in place prior to making the loan.

Title insurance companies conduct a thorough search of public records to discern the *chain of title* to the home and whether any encumbrances appear on the title. If the search confirms that the seller is the true owner of the home, and no recorded encumbrance exists that would diminish the buyer's claim to the title of the home, the title insurance company will issue a *binder*. The binder states that once the premium has been paid and the closing has occurred, a policy will be issued in the name of the buyer and any secured lender.

Remember: Title insurance companies do not represent either the buyer or the seller. They only present facts to the buyer and the seller and, if desired, provide insurance of title to the buyer. Although this can change from area to area, the cost of title insurance is generally a few hundred dollars for a typical home. This cost can be paid by either party, or divided equally, depending on what is agreed upon in the purchase agreement.

Some areas do not allow for title insurance. In such a case, a real estate attorney would then review the *abstract* of the home. The abstract is a written history of the transfer of the home from person to person over the years. If the attorney is convinced that the seller has good title, he will issue a formal opinion to that effect. In general, title insurance companies have proven more cost effective and efficient in insuring titles.

Often the question arises of why the buyer should obtain a survey if title insurance is also procured. Most title insurance policies have an exception in their coverage as follows:

> Any discrepancies or conflicts in boundary lines, any shortages in any area, or any encroachment or overlapping of improvements are not included in the coverage of this policy.

So if a buyer suspects a potential problem with the exact boundary lines of the home, he should definitely obtain a survey as well as title insurance.

Lenders Institutional lenders in a home purchase can also be a source of professional assistance. Since the majority of real estate sales depend upon the buyer being able to borrow the necessary funds to purchase the home, the lender needs to make sure that the buyer is receiving good and valid title prior to making the loan.

If the seller does not have good and valid title, the lender will not have security for the loan being made to the buyer. Therefore, the lender is in essence representing the buyer at closing because the lender is just as concerned about the buyer having good title as is the buyer.

SELLER'S PREPARATION FOR CLOSING

Evidence of Title

The seller's most important obligation at the time of closing is to provide adequate evidence of title. Achieving this rests upon the seller's ability to provide proof that he is the owner of the home and has the legal ability and authority to transfer it. This evidence must be provided to the buyer's satisfaction as set forth in the purchase agreement.

There are several ways the homeowner can provide evidence of title to the buyer. These have been discussed, and include an attorney's opinion or title insurance. The purchase agreement should clearly state which method is acceptable to the buyer.

Removal of Liens or Other Title Encumbrances

Sometimes a review of the history of the title to the home discloses certain liens, mortgages, or encumbrances of record. These could include judgment liens in the name of the homeowner, delinquent real estate taxes, or past due income taxes that have become liens on the home.

It becomes the seller's obligation to remove these encumbrances so that the closing can occur. As previously mentioned, an attorney will often have to be procured to remove these encumbrances, especially if they are the result of prior judicial action against the seller. Other common types of judicial action that may create a lien on the home include a judgment against the seller, non-payment of child support or an existing obligation to pay child support by the seller, or inheritance tax due on the home not paid by a previous title holder.

Existing mortgages are another type of encumbrance that has to be removed before the buyer is obligated to purchase the home. Of course, this is not true if the buyer is assuming the existing loan and mortgage. The existing mortgage and note is generally paid off at the time of closing with the money received by the seller from the buyer for the sale price of the home.

Other types of judgment liens also have to be removed, usually by having the homeowner pay off whatever amount is owed. The judgment creditor usually files a satisfaction or release with the appropriate court to indicate that the judgment lien has been extinguished.

Some states require that any real estate in the name of a child support obligor have a lien against it in the amount of the due and owing child support. The child support obligor may be totally current with his payments, yet the lien will still exist and must be removed prior to the closing. A judge will usually be required to sign a court order before the lien is removed and the closing can occur. If the child support obligor is not current with his payments, he will most likely have to pay the arrearages before the lien can be removed by court order.

If any of the previously mentioned liens or encumbrances cannot be removed prior to the time of closing, certain other methods for curing title defects are available. If, for instance, a judgment lien in the amount of $5,000 is against the home, the seller may agree to a $5,000 reduction in the purchase price rather than attempt to satisfy the lien and delay the closing. Since the judgment lien amount and the amount of the reduction of the purchase price of the home are equal, the buyer is not necessarily losing anything. Of course, it is up to the buyer to decide whether to agree to a price reduction or require the seller to remove the judgment lien before the deed is transferred.

It is also up to the homeowner to have the deed ready at the time of closing in a form acceptable to the buyer. The type of deed required from the seller is stated in the purchase agreement. Usually the buyer is allowed to review a copy of the deed prior to the closing in the event that there are any problems with it that can be corrected before the day of closing.

The rule then with regard to the deed can be stated as follows: The seller prepares, and the buyer reviews. The original executed deed is not presented to the buyer until the date of closing. If it is executed prior to closing, it will not be released to the buyer until the purchase price has been received. The different types of deeds and how they are used are discussed in Chapter 5.

Repairs and Inspection   Sometimes the purchase agreement has a contingency stating that the homeowner needs to make certain repairs in the home before the buyer becomes obligated to close. For example, the seller may have to repair a garage door to the satisfaction of the buyer, or he may have to repair or replace a termite-infested deck prior to closing.

It is the seller's responsibility to make sure that these repairs are made prior to the closing date. The buyer should insist that he inspect these repairs prior to closing to make sure that everything is completed to the buyer's satisfaction.

Lease Assignments   If the home being sold is currently being used as rental property and involves existing tenants, the seller needs to prepare an *assignment of leasehold interest*. This assignment is a separate document that the seller signs, giving the buyer any and all rights (and obligations) to all rental contracts with current tenants in the home.

Lien Waiver Affidavit   Another obligation of the homeowner is that, subsequent to the signing of the purchase agreement but prior to closing, he is to provide an execution of *lien waiver affidavit*. If a title insurance company is involved, this will be required before the title insurance policy can be issued.

A lien waiver affidavit generally provides written evidence that the homeowner has not authorized a third party to perform any type of permanent improvement on the home within a certain period of time prior to closing, without that party being paid in full. This is necessary because in most states if permanent improvements are made upon real estate, and the contractor or suppliers doing the work have not been paid, they may file a lien on the real estate. This lien would remain on the title to the home after closing and ultimately have to be paid by the buyer.

Mortgage Payoff Most homes being sold are subject to an existing mortgage. These mortgage balances need to be paid at a time prior to closing, unless the buyer is assuming the existing mortgage.

Generally, the seller can arrange to have a specific payoff figure in advance, with a per diem figure thereafter. This arrangement allows the payoff figure to be adjusted accordingly if the scheduled closing date is delayed. As already discussed, the existing mortgage on the home is usually paid from the sale proceeds received by the seller.

Corporate/Partnership Authority If the seller of the home happens to be a corporation rather than an individual, the seller would need to have a *corporate resolution*, which specifically authorizes the sale of the property. If the home is owned by a partnership, there must be some type of written evidence on behalf of one of the general partners that the transfer is authorized by the partnership.

Without this type of documentation, the individual ostensibly signing on behalf of either the corporation or the partnership may not actually have the legal authority to do so, and the sale may be rescinded (retroactively canceled) by the seller sometime after closing. The purchase agreement should have a provision that the seller will provide any necessary documentation to establish that the seller is authorizing the transfer of the property. This is only important if the seller is a partnership or corporation.

Termite Inspection Another document that the homeowner should procure prior to closing is a wood infestation certificate by a qualified termite inspection company. The certificate indicates and guarantees that a termite inspection has been conducted and that no such defect has been found, or if found has been corrected to the buyer's satisfaction. This type of certificate is a standard contingency in most purchase agreements and will almost always be required by the lender at closing.

Review of Documentation It is always a good idea to have all the documentation required of the homeowner at closing reviewed by the buyer or the buyer's attorney prior to the actual time of closing. If an objection to the documentation is made, either with regard to substance or form, the homeowner is typically given an adequate opportunity to correct any errors or omissions. With all contingencies met, the closing can then proceed and the home be sold.

In the Appendix is an example of a Seller's Settlement Sheet, which typifies the different charges and credits that come into play with regard to the seller at closing. After all the applicable costs are subtracted and the purchase price of the home is factored in, the net amount due to the seller results.

BUYER'S PREPARATION FOR CLOSING

Obtaining Financing

If the buyer is not able to pay cash for the home, the major hurdle he must overcome to close is obtaining financing. Indeed, most purchase agreements have as their primary contingency the buyer's ability to obtain a loan at acceptable terms. It is implied within the purchase agreement, and should be expressed if at all possible, that the buyer must attempt to obtain the loan in good faith and with all due diligence.

Credit Concerns

When a buyer is searching for a loan to comply with the specifics of the purchase agreement, often certain *credit defects* arise. These credit defects can take a number of forms.

For instance, if the buyer has an unacceptable amount of long-term debts or judgment liens against him, or is not making enough in the way of annual or monthly income to justify the monthly payment that would be involved in the home purchase, the lender may refuse to make the loan.

At that time, if possible, the buyer will have to do whatever is reasonably necessary to correct the situation for the loan to be approved and the closing to occur. Sometimes this is not possible, as in the case of annual income or the like, and the purchase agreement no longer has any legal effect.

If real estate brokers are involved in the sale, most potential buyers will be *pre-qualified*. This means that, in the opinion of the broker, the buyer would be able to qualify for the loan to close the sale if a purchase agreement is agreed upon for the approximate asking price of the home.

If an insurmountable credit concern arises after the execution of the purchase agreement, and the buyer is not able to obtain the loan to close, the seller would then put the home back on the market. It is always a good idea for the homeowner to keep close track of the buyer's loan application process to determine whether the buyer is having trouble procuring the necessary loan. This way, the homeowner may be able to keep other possible buyers interested if the loan is not obtained.

Correcting Title Defects

If the buyer obtains the loan to purchase the home, the buyer's next focus will be on the deed that will be transferred at closing. As previously mentioned, the seller must provide evidence of good title at the time of closing. However, it is incumbent upon the buyer to decide whether good title is available to him at the time of closing.

The buyer should never wait until after closing to correct any title defects. The buyer has the most leverage prior to closing, when the funds for the purchase are not yet received by the seller.

As also mentioned in the previous section, title concerns are important to the lender. If there is a problem with the title to the home, the lender's security interest may not be adequately protected. It should be remembered, however, that in some circumstances the title may have certain defects that minimize the buyer's interest but do not necessarily affect the lender's security. An example of this type of defect would be a minor encroachment on a boundary line to the home.

Property Inspection The buyer should make, prior to closing, an inspection of the premises. This inspection is called the *final walk-through*.

Since it is not unusual for a substantial period of time to pass from the date the purchase agreement is signed to the date of closing, the buyer needs to take a final review or walk-through of the home to assure himself that the premises have not been damaged.

The buyer should never assume that the home is in the same condition at closing as it was when the purchase agreement was signed. An inspection after the closing has occurred may leave the buyer in a position merely to request, rather than require, the seller to correct any defects. Again, the buyer's maximum leverage is prior to, not after, closing.

Remember that the discovery of a defect in the home does not mean that the buyer is not obligated to close. Instead, the seller has a right to cure any such defect within a reasonable period of time. However, this rule does not generally apply to a substantial or material defect that causes a severe reduction in the value of the home.

Boundary Lines Sometimes a buyer conducts a survey prior to closing. A survey company will specifically provide to the buyer the exact boundaries of the property. Often the exact property lines are not where a row of hedges or a fence may be, as the buyer may presume by walking around the home site.

If the survey reveals an encroachment by a neighboring property or an *easement* that may impinge on how the buyer wishes to use the property, these impediments should be pointed out to the seller prior to closing. The seller can, if possible, then correct the encroachments or easements. If such a correction is not possible, then the seller may be forced to reduce the purchase price to an amount reflecting these defects. Easements are defined and discussed in Chapter 9.

Leases and Other Rights of the Buyer If any leases are to be assumed by the buyer with any existing tenants to the home, the seller should provide copies of any existing leases to the buyer prior to closing. As already mentioned, an assignment of the leasehold interest needs to be executed by the seller at the time of closing. Any questions regarding the liability or assumptive rights of the buyer should be presented and corrected between the buyer and the seller prior to closing.

Hazard Insurance Whether or not the buyer is purchasing the home without the assistance of a lender, the buyer should always obtain hazard insurance on the home to take effect at the date of closing. If a lender is involved, this insurance will be required, and proof of it will need to be made at time of closing before the loan is made.

The lender usually specifies the necessary type of coverage. The lender is named as a co-insured, usually up to the amount of the loan.

Closing Funds The seller is entitled to the purchase price at the time of closing. The money due the seller reflects all credits due the buyer for earnest money deposits, tax adjustments, insurance, and utilities.

The buyer will most likely need to have certified funds (a certified check or cashier's check) for the precise amount due at the time of closing. Generally, the closing secretary and/or lender will know the exact amount needed at closing and so advise the buyer. Very few sellers will transfer the deed unless the funds are certified. The purchase agreement will usually state this as a requirement.

Corporate/Partnership Purchase Authority If the buyer of the home is a corporation or partnership, specific written authority to purchase the property should be made available to the seller at closing. This will usually be in the form of a partnership authority statement or corporate resolution. This provides the necessary evidence to the seller showing that the buyer has the legal authority to act on behalf of the entity he represents. This basically ensures that the closing cannot be rescinded at a later date by other members of the corporation or partnership.

Settlement Sheet The buyer also can use a settlement sheet to assist in determining all applicable debits and credits pursuant to the purchase. In the Appendix is an example of a Buyer's Settlement Sheet.

REAL ESTATE SETTLEMENT PROCEDURES ACT

Under a federal law entitled the Real Estate Settlement Procedures Act, lenders must disclose certain information about various aspects of the loan to buyers of residential property. Lenders are also prohibited from engaging in certain types of other practices.

Description and Applicability of Real Estate Settlement Procedures Act The Real Estate Settlement Procedures Act (also known as RESPA) applies to first mortgage loans made for residential real estate, including one- to four-family properties, cooperatives, condominiums, and mobile homes. The Act only applies to purchases in which the lender (other than the seller) obtains a first mortgage as security for the loan. A purchase money mortgage, in which the seller takes back a mortgage to secure an unpaid purchase price that the seller otherwise provides, is not subject to the provisions of RESPA.

The requirements contained in RESPA are applicable only to lenders involved in *federally related mortgage loans*. The definition of *federally related* is very broad and includes any lender whose funds are federally insured or regulated, or that pertain to interstate commerce. This covers almost all standard mortgage companies, banks, and savings and loans involved in residential real estate mortgage lending.

The premise behind RESPA is that a borrower trying to obtain a mortgage loan needs full and clear information from a potential lender in order to make an informed decision about whether or not to procure the loan.

Settlement Costs Booklet A lender falling under the RESPA umbrella must provide every loan applicant with a settlement costs booklet. This booklet needs to be provided to the potential borrower when the loan application is made, or mailed to the applicant within three business days thereafter.

The booklet contains various information concerning the real estate purchase process, including certain factors that the potential borrower needs to disclose prior to obtaining a loan with a particular lender. Also contained in the booklet is information about the buyer's legal rights, settlement services offered, and advantage or disadvantage of escrow accounts. The entire booklet is geared toward educating the borrower to allow him to decide to proceed with the loan if he believes it is in his best interest.

Good Faith Estimate of Settlement Charges Under RESPA, the lender must provide a borrower with a good faith estimate of any settlement charges for which the borrower will be responsible if he is approved for the home loan. This good faith estimate does not have to be exact, and may in fact indicate a range of figures. However, as with the settlement costs booklet, this good faith estimate of the costs must be provided at the time of the loan application or within three business days thereafter.

The charges that need to be presented to the potential borrower include estimated credit report fees, loan origination fee, appraisal fees, title search fees, surveys, and document preparation charges. RESPA allows for changes in these estimates if the changes are merely a reflection in the volatility of the marketplace between the time the application is made and the time of closing.

Uniform Settlement Statement Another requirement of RESPA is that the lender must make available to the borrower at or prior to closing a form commonly known as the *uniform settlement statement*. This is, in essence, a summary of the buyer's and the seller's transaction and includes a complete itemization of both settlement charges allocated to the buyer and the seller, respectively.

Should the information contained in the uniform settlement statement not be available prior to closing, the lender may give it to the buyer after closing, but only if the requirement is waived in writing by the buyer at the time of closing. Even with this waiver, the uniform settlement statement must be forwarded to the buyer at the lender's earliest possible convenience.

Please note that the lender is not required to provide a uniform settlement statement to the buyer when there are no buyer settlement charges, or when the settlement charges have been communicated to the buyer at the time the loan application was made and have not changed in amount. Regardless, the lender must provide the buyer within three business days after closing an itemized list of all charges for services provided. In all transactions covered by the RESPA, a uniform settlement statement is absolutely required and cannot be waived. (There is an example of a HUD-1 Settlement Statement in the Appendix.)

RESPA-Prohibited Practices The Real Estate Settlement Procedures Act also prohibits certain practices that have led to unnecessary closing costs to the buyer. RESPA specifically prohibits kickbacks. For instance, if a lender requires that an attorney review the closing documentation on behalf of the buyer, and that attorney gives a percentage of his fee charged to the buyer back to the lender, a kickback situation arises. This type of practice is specifically prohibited by RESPA.

In addition, any charges that cannot be attributed to a specific act or service are prohibited. An individual who has a legitimate grievance under RESPA prohibitions can potentially recover three times the amount that was illegally obtained. If a buyer feels that he was not provided with all the necessary information during the loan process under the RESPA mandates, he should immediately consult with an attorney or contact the state attorney general's office.

Post-Closing Procedures Immediately subsequent to the closing, the deed transferred to the buyer needs to be recorded in the applicable public office in the county in which the home is located. The security document, such as the mortgage or deed of trust, also needs to be recorded to evidence that the home is subject to a security interest. Furthermore, any documents indicating that previous mortgages or liens in the name of the seller have been paid should also be filed as a matter of public record.

Most title insurance companies will not issue the title insurance policy until after closing. Prior to that time, the title insurance company issues a preliminary binder or title commitment, which amounts to a statement indicating that a title insurance policy will be issued if certain requirements are met and the closing does occur.

After closing, the buyer will be entitled to possession of the home. All keys, garage door openers, and other badges of occupancy are transferred to the buyer. If a post-closing occupancy agreement is involved, it needs to be signed. These agreements and their effect on closing are discussed in Chapter 5.

LAND INSTALLMENT SALES CONTRACT CLOSING

As already discussed, a typical land installment sales contract is where the buyer makes periodic payments over an extended period of time before the seller is obligated to transfer the deed. This kind of arrangement usually makes it unnecessary for the buyer to obtain a loan to purchase the home. Also, it is typical for the buyer to occupy the home during the term of the contract.

There are generally two closings to a land installment sales contract. The first closing occurs when the contract is executed and the payments from the buyer commence. The second closing is when the last payment is paid by the buyer to the seller, who then transfers the deed to the buyer.

If, however, the buyer is unable to make the last installment payment without first obtaining a loan, as in the case of a large balloon payment due at the end of the contract period, a lender usually comes into the picture and the second closing of a land installment sales contract is analogous to a cash for deed type closing.

ESCROW CLOSINGS

In some areas of the country, sales are closed in escrow. A deed is deposited by the seller with a third party (escrow agent) to be delivered to the buyer upon payment of the purchase price to the escrow agent.

The subject of the escrow transaction is the deed to the home. The deed is held by the escrow agent during the term of the transaction. The buyer and the seller agree in the purchase agreement to close the sale in escrow by appointing an escrow agent to handle the mechanical details of the closing.

The seller executes an acceptable deed in compliance with the purchase agreement and forwards the deed to the escrow agent. The buyer then obtains the necessary purchase price from a lender or other source and forwards the funds to the escrow agent. When the escrow agent receives these items, in satisfactory form and amount pursuant to the terms of the purchase agreement, the deed is forwarded to the buyer and the money is forwarded to the seller.

In order to have a legally enforceable escrow closing agreement, the following elements are necessary:

- ❏ a purchase agreement for the sale of the home
- ❏ a valid deed from the seller to the buyer
- ❏ the delivery of the deed to an escrow agent
- ❏ an escrow agent with the power to handle the escrow closing
- ❏ a separate oral or written escrow agreement

Without the existence of these necessary elements, a valid escrow does not exist, and the escrow closing can be legally canceled by either the buyer or the seller.

The main advantage of an escrow closing is the protection it affords from intervening liens. In a typical situation, the escrow agent is to record the deed immediately upon receipt of the purchase price. This minimizes the risk of any intervening creditors of the seller attempting to obtain an encumbrance on the title, thus complicating or delaying the closing.

Escrow closings are also used to prevent the closing from not occurring due to a change of circumstances between the date of the purchase agreement and the time the deed is to be transferred. These circumstances include a change of mind by either the buyer or the seller; death of the buyer or the seller; or the loss of legal ability to contract (such as intervening mental incompetency) by one of the parties.

If any existing objectionable liens or encumbrances to the title are discovered during the period of escrow, the escrow agent may be given the authority to apply a portion of proceeds from the purchase price to remove the liens.

The following diagram illustrates how an escrow closing is designed to work:

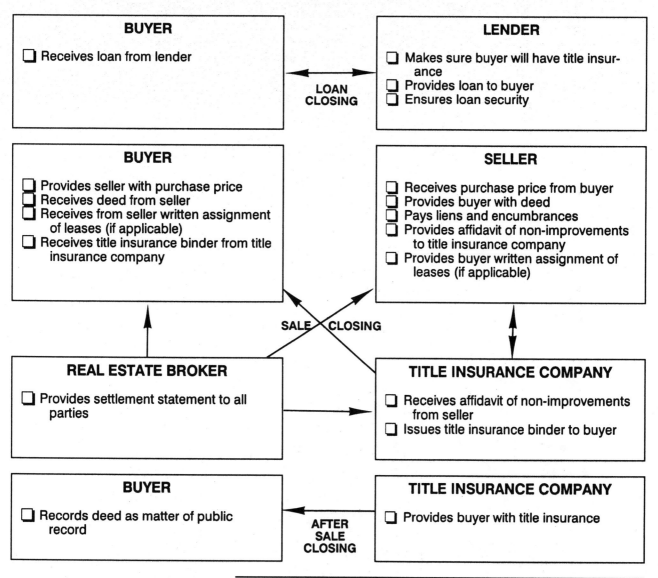

Events occurring at the loan closing and during and after the sale closing of a real estate transaction.

DEED OF TRUST CLOSINGS The purchase agreement often provides that the buyer must obtain a loan to purchase the home. Once the loan is made, the lender receives an interest in the home to secure the loan. In a mortgage situation, the deed to the home is transferred to the buyer, subject to the mortgage given by the buyer to the lender in exchange for the money necessary to purchase the home.

In a deed of trust closing, however, instead of executing a mortgage in favor of the lender, the buyer transfers title at closing to a third party (trustee) for the term of indebtedness. The deed transferred to the trustee is known as a *deed of trust*. Due to the major differences between a mortgage and a deed of trust as to enforcement, the buyer at a deed of trust closing may be required to execute an acknowledgment of deed of trust document. See Chapter 3 for a complete discussion regarding the acknowledgment of a deed of trust.

5

Related Topics to the Home Purchase

Several other topics related to the purchase or sale of a home need to be understood for a complete understanding of the legalities entailed in the transaction.

LISTING AGREEMENTS The majority of homes in this country are sold using the services of a real estate broker. When the homeowner has made the decision to sell, a real estate broker is often contacted, and a listing agreement is negotiated and executed. The various types of listing agreements and their effect on the sale were defined and reviewed in Chapter 1. This section expands further upon the topic of listing agreements.

Requirements of the Listing Agreement No matter what particular type of listing agreement is used, it constitutes a legally binding contract between a homeowner and a real estate broker, in which the broker is attempting to locate a suitable buyer on terms that have been previously set by the seller. Once this acceptable buyer has been procured, a fee is deemed to have been earned by the broker. This fee generally amounts to a certain percentage of the sale price of the home. The commission is never set by law, but is totally negotiable between the seller and the listing broker.

The listing agreement should always contain the following elements:

- ❑ the amount of compensation to the broker
- ❑ the period of time that the listing agreement will be in effect
- ❑ at what particular point the commission is deemed to be earned
- ❑ a description of the home attempting to be sold
- ❑ the scope of authority the broker has in locating a suitable buyer

It should be noted that these elements are preferred and suggested but not absolutely necessary in all circumstances to create a binding listing agreement. The law will sometimes infer or imply these elements from the circumstances surrounding the transaction.

Multiple Listing Service Within any given geographical area, there is always a market of available homes that are listed by different brokers. To allow for the effective exchange of information pertaining to these particular listings, a brokerage agreement exists between real estate brokers who, as members of a multiple listing service, make this information available to one another.

These multiple listing exchanges become crucial as a *shared listing* agreement, and, accordingly, the otherwise competing brokers agree to divide the commission received for negotiating the sale. That is, if one broker is working with a particular buyer and matches that buyer up with a home currently for sale through another broker, the commission agreed upon in the listing agreement is divided between the brokers. How the commission is split depends upon local custom or standard of practice.

Commissions A real estate broker does not generally receive his commission until the closing has occurred. However, there are certain situations in which the broker would be legally entitled to a commission even if the sale does not close.

For example, if the homeowner changes his mind and refuses, for no justifiable or legal reason, to otherwise sell the home to an acceptable buyer, the broker will in all likelihood be legally entitled to a commission and will have a legal cause of action to recover the commission from the seller. Also, if the homeowner's spouse refuses to execute any necessary closing documents (such as the deed), the broker would be equally entitled to his commission.

If there happen to be defects in the seller's title to the home that he does not correct prior to closing, the broker would also be entitled to his commission even if the closing fails to occur.

Any type of actual fraud committed by the homeowner during the transaction that results in the buyer not completing the sale will entitle the broker to a legal right to recover his commission.

For example, suppose the homeowner has stated throughout the sale process to both the buyer and the listing broker that there have been no water problems whatsoever in the basement of the home. Then evidence of water damage or leakage is discovered in the home just prior to closing, and the buyer refuses to close. The homeowner's fraud, which resulted in the rescission of the purchase agreement, does not negate the broker's right to his commission.

The broker would be owed a commission even though the sale does not close if the seller does not deliver the home within a reasonable period of time surrounding the date of possession stated in the purchase agreement.

If the homeowner insists on certain restrictions or terms not mentioned in the listing agreement (such as refusing to sell the home to a certain racial or minority group), the broker is entitled to his commission if the buyer is otherwise ready, willing, and able.

As a practical matter, very few brokers pursue their cause of action for commissions if, in fact, the commission has not been received at a formal closing. The bad public relations aspect of having to sue for a commission generally outweighs the amount of money involved. So, although in theory a commission can be earned even though a formal closing did not transpire, rarely is a commission received unless the closing is achieved.

Also keep in mind that if the commission is earned but not paid, the broker cannot legally place a lien on the home for the commission amount unless the listing agreement specifically includes a provision indicating that the broker may take such action. Nor can the broker force payment of the commission by doing anything to prevent the sale of the home. The broker's only option to recover his earned commission is to take his case to court.

Revocation or Termination of the Listing Agreement

Revocation or termination of a listing agreement can occur in a variety of ways. The most common is by allowing the time period specified in the listing agreement to expire. That is, if a ready, willing, and able buyer has not been located by the broker during the term of the listing agreement, the broker is not entitled to a commission.

It should be kept in mind that if the listing broker locates an acceptable buyer for the home, but the buyer has not entered into a purchase agreement when the listing expires, the law usually allows the broker his commission. The rationale for this legal theory is that the broker initiated a series of events that culminated in the buyer purchasing the home.

All listing agreements should have a specific time frame. Thirty, sixty, or ninety days for a listing period are not uncommon. However, if the listing agreement makes no reference whatsoever to a specific expiration date, the listing broker's authority lapses after a reasonable period of time. What constitutes a reasonable period of time is dictated by the circumstances surrounding the creation of the listing agreement on a case-by-case basis.

If no duration of the listing agreement is specified, the homeowner retains the right to revoke the agreement at any time, so long as the broker has not already located an acceptable buyer. However, any such revocation by the homeowner must be in good faith; that is, it must not be made in an effort to circumvent the obligation of paying a commission.

The listing agreement will also be effectively revoked if the homeowner can demonstrate that the broker has abandoned the listing agreement. Abandonment in this context can be defined as the total lack of any effort exercised by the broker in an attempt to sell the home. The homeowner and broker can also mutually agree to cancel the listing agreement.

Other circumstances in which the listing agreement can be revoked include the homeowner declaring bankruptcy, dying, or becoming legally incompetent. Also, if the broker's company declares bankruptcy, effectively goes out of business, or for whatever reason ceases to exist as a viable entity, the listing agreement will be negated and automatically revoked.

If the home is destroyed during the period of the listing agreement, the obligations contained in the agreement will no longer be in effect. Any substantial change or material variation in the outside restrictions or forces that have an effect on the use or condition of the home also renders the listing agreement null and void. For example, a change in the zoning status of the home during the term of the listing agreement usually has such a major effect on the ability to utilize and sell the home that the listing agreement will be effectively terminated.

DEEDS

A deed to a home is the written instrument by which one person or entity conveys the property to another. Please recognize the important difference between the terms *deed* and *title*.

In essence, when reference is made to the *title* to a home, it generally means that a particular individual owns or has ownership rights to that home. The term *title* is equated with ownership.

However, when reference is made to the *deed* to the home, the deed is considered the actual, tangible written document of ownership evidence of the home. That is, title is equated with ownership while the deed evidences title.

Elements of a Deed

There are several necessary elements that are required for any deed to constitute a valid and legal instrument to transfer a home. First of all, every deed must have a *grantor*. The grantor is the individual or entity selling or conveying the home. The individual who is transferring the home must not be declared legally incompetent, insane, or otherwise be legally prevented from making the transfer.

The second essential element in any deed is an identifiable *grantee*. The grantee is the receiver of what is being transferred, that is, the buyer or recipient of the home. All that is legally necessary is that the grantee be sufficiently identifiable. If a minor misspelling of a name is contained in the deed, this is not necessarily fatal. If it can be shown that the name on the deed was not the name of the intended grantee, the intended grantee will in any event be able to prove that the grantor intended to transfer the home to the correct individual. The controlling factor in any conveying of a home is the intent of the grantor, regardless of any mistakes made in the deed itself with regard to any incorrect spelling or misnomer of the grantee. A grantee does not usually execute the deed nor is he required to do so.

All deeds must contain some type of language of conveyance. Several terms are considered sufficient, including the following: convey, transfer, release, or sell. Without such words of conveyance, the deed is not considered a valid transfer instrument.

The deed must sufficiently describe the property being transferred, usually by way of a legal description. A street address can also be used in conjunction with the legal description.

The signature of the grantor is essential to the validity of the deed. Any type of forgery by the grantor generally renders the transaction null and void and conveys no interest in the home. Grantors can designate an agent or a power of attorney to sign the deed for them.

If a corporation, partnership, or other type of business entity is transferring the property, a corporate resolution or partnership statement, granting the individual the necessary prerequisite power to transfer the property, should accompany the deed.

The element of *consideration* is not necessary for the effective transfer of a home. Consideration is legally defined as the price paid or services rendered, transferred, or exchanged for the home conveyed. That is, something is given from the buyer to the seller in exchange for the seller transferring the property to the buyer.

Deeds often refer to *one dollar and other valuable consideration* to indicate that a transfer of consideration did occur. However, the fact that no consideration was given for a home does not necessarily invalidate the transfer. The grantor may legally give the home to the grantee without any monetary consideration whatsoever.

Only if the grantor is making a transfer of the home for the purpose of removing the property from his name to avoid creditors will the transfer of the property possibly be set aside for lack of consideration. It is always good practice to refer to some type of consideration in the deed itself.

Finally, the grantor must intend actually to pass title and surrender control of the deed. Without these two elements of intent and surrender, the transfer of the home will not be effective.

For instance, if the grantor intended to transfer title, but for whatever reason the grantee never received the deed to the home, the transfer of the home has not been effective. By the same token, if for whatever reason a buyer comes into possession of an otherwise valid deed without the grantor actually intending to surrender the deed to the buyer, no valid transfer has occurred. The intent to transfer ownership must always be coupled with the actual relinquishment of the deed to constitute a valid and legal conveyance of the home.

Warranty Deed The most common type of deed used to transfer ownership interest in a home is called a *warranty deed*. A warranty deed is a deed that conveys title to the buyer and makes certain legally implied promises or covenants within the deed itself.

The first covenant implicitly contained in a warranty deed is called the *covenant of seisin*. The covenant of seisin means that the grantor is promising that he has the legal right to convey the property. The covenant of seisin is, in essence, providing that the seller has good title to the home and has no legal prohibitions against transferring it to the buyer.

A second covenant contained in a warranty deed is called the *covenant against encumbrances*. This covenant states that there are no encumbrances, mortgages, or liens on the property except those otherwise stated in the deed or a matter of public record or otherwise made known to the buyer. Indeed, a written reference is almost always contained in the warranty deed itself that an exception to this covenant includes all encumbrances that are a matter of public record and otherwise known by the buyer.

The third type of covenant contained in a warranty deed is called the *covenant of quiet enjoyment*. This covenant means that the buyer will not be evicted or disturbed in his enjoyment or possession of the home by a person having paramount or better title to the property.

Two things need to be mentioned with regard to warranty deeds. First, the aforementioned covenants contained in a warranty deed are deemed to *run with the land*. That is, they are binding not only upon the seller in one particular transaction, but they also allow future buyers who take title from the present owner to go back and enforce these covenants against any of the previous owners, provided that the previous seller also conveyed the home by a warranty deed.

Second, even though it appears from the above discussion that a buyer who receives a warranty deed from a homeowner is pretty safe in having good and valid title, title insurance should still be procured any time a home is purchased. Even though the seller is making these various implied promises with regard to the soundness of the title, if the seller cannot be found, has no assets, or is otherwise unable to make good on the promises, the buyer has no practical recourse if a third party claims an enforceable legal interest in the home. This is why title insurance is required by all lenders even though the home is being transferred by warranty deed.

Bargain and Sale Deed

A *bargain and sale deed* conveys the home but does not include any warranties of title that would otherwise be conveyed as in a warranty deed. If a buyer should obtain title to the home through a sheriff's sale on a foreclosed piece of property, that person is obtaining a bargain and sale deed. A seller transferring title by a bargain and sale deed is stating that he has authority to transfer title to the home, but makes no warranties whatsoever about any encumbrances on the property or any third party claims that may be made against it.

Another example of bargain and sale deed is one in which an executor of an estate transfers title to a home to a beneficiary under the terms of a will or laws of inheritance. In this case, the beneficiary is obtaining title to the home, but the grantor is not making any promises or guarantees that a third party may not have a claim against the title or have a lien or mortgage against the home.

Quitclaim Deed

A *quitclaim deed* is a deed used in situations where the seller is only conveying any interest that he may have in the home. The seller does not legally promise or imply that he has any ownership interest in the home. If the seller actually has no interest in the home, then no interest whatsoever is transferred to the buyer and the buyer has no legal recourse against the seller.

A quitclaim deed is often used to remove outside or potential third party interests in the title to a home. If a particular third party has a potential interest in the home, thus creating a cloud on a title, he may transfer any interest he may have (with or without consideration) to any grantee by using a quitclaim deed.

Quitclaim deeds are also used in divorce settlements in which one spouse is decreed to transfer his or her interest in the marital home to the other spouse according to the terms of the property settlement. One spouse merely executes a quitclaim deed to the other spouse to remove his or her name from the title to the home.

You should remember that a grantee obtaining ownership by a quitclaim deed obtains no legal rights of recourse against the grantor should the grantee not obtain clear title to the home. When a quitclaim deed is utilized, the grantor is not promising that he is in fact conveying title, but only that any title interest he may have is being transferred.

Recording of the Deed It is not necessary to record a deed in a public office to transfer the ownership interest in a home or to make the transfer valid. Recording of the deed is standard and wise practice, however, in order to provide public notice (also called *constructive notice*) of the transaction for the benefit and protection of the homeowner.

If an otherwise valid deed is not recorded, and subsequently the home is sold by the former owner to another buyer who had no notice of the previous sale, a title dispute would arise between the two buyers, generally because of the failure of the original buyer to record the deed. Hence, the recording of the deed is used as a safeguard for the buyer to protect his interest against any subsequent transfers of the same property by the previous owner.

Execution and Attestation of the Deed Recognize that the signature of the grantor on the deed may not be required to be notarized or witnessed, depending upon local law. Generally, however, a signature of witnesses and/or the verification of a notary public adds to the legal validity of the deed. This witnessing and notarizing is called an *attestation* and creates a legal presumption of correctness that may become critical if the deed's validity is ever challenged.

TYPES OF OWNERSHIP

There are several different methods of owning a home. The particular type of ownership and its inherent legal ramifications are contained in the deed. A general discussion of the various different types of ownership is included in this section.

Fee Simple Absolute *Fee simple absolute*, also known as *fee simple*, can be defined as the most extensive interest in the property that the homeowner can possess. It is potentially indefinite in duration. Most homes are held in fee simple ownership. The holder of a fee simple title to a home possesses all rights commonly associated with property or ownership. These include the right of possession, the right of disposition, and the right to potentially limit future use of the home.

The necessary terminology to create a fee simple absolute ownership interest is to convey the property to the grantee *and his heirs*. Thus, the granting clause in a deed will generally be worded as follows:

"Lot Seven (7), Block Ten (10), Bent Tree Subdivision, to John Smith and his heirs." This creates a fee simple absolute ownership in the property.

Life Estate   A *life estate* can be defined as a period of ownership in a home, limited in duration or measured by the life of another. A life estate is typically measured by the life of the owner of the home, but it can be determined by the life of some third party if so designated in the deed.

A life estate, when granted to an individual, gives that person all the rights to the home as a fee simple owner, during the life of the owner. Upon the death of the owner, the life estate terminates, and the home generally reverts back to the ownership of the grantor.

Life estates are often used as an estate device to avoid inheritance or estate taxes. Obviously, a person would have limited success in attempting to sell his life estate interest, as the buyer would only be the legal owner of the property during the life of the seller.

Dower   *Dower* is defined as the legal interest one spouse has in a home that is solely in the name of the other spouse at the time of his or her death.

Divorce terminates the right to a dower interest. Many states no longer recognize the dower concept; however, some jurisdictions still recognize it as a legal theory of ownership rights, and the homeowner should be aware of its possible existence, especially with regard to estate planning.

Joint Tenancy   *Joint tenancy* is a type of co-ownership in a home. The prime feature of joint tenancy ownership is the *right of survivorship*. When one of the owners under a joint tenancy dies, that person's interest in the home automatically passes to the surviving joint tenant. Most typically, spouses own their home as joint tenants. The terminology in a deed that creates a joint tenancy would be as follows: "To John Jones and Mary Jones, as joint tenants with rights of survivorship, and not as tenants in common."

The advantage of owning a home as a joint tenant is the automatic transfer provision entailed in the right of survivorship. That is, no probate or estate action is usually required to have the home remain in the name of the surviving joint tenant.

All joint tenants are legally presumed to have an equal and undivided interest in possession and title to the property.

Tenancy in Common   A *tenancy in common* type of ownership of a home can be defined as a concurrent ownership in which each particular tenant in common possesses an undivided right to the property.

Like joint tenants, each tenant in common has an undivided right to possess the property. The prime difference between a tenant in common and a joint tenant is that a tenant in common, upon his death, will have his interest in the property transferred to his heirs, not necessarily to the surviving tenant in common.

Tenants in common contain no right of survivorship provision and, accordingly, are generally used by two or more individuals or entities who wish to own property together yet retain dispositive control over their respective interests.

Tenancy by the Entirety   *Tenancy by the entirety* is defined as the co-ownership of a home solely between spouses. Only approximately one-half of the country recognizes tenancy by the entirety. It only can occur between husband and wife, and, upon the death of either, the survivor remains as the sole owner.

The right of survivorship by the tenancy in entirety is very similar to that of joint tenancy. Recognize, however, that tenancy by the entirety home ownership cannot exist except between spouses. This is not required of joint tenants with rights of survivorship.

EARLY-LATE OCCUPANCY AGREEMENTS   The purchase of a home usually allows the buyer to have immediate possession at the time of closing. However, if the circumstances of the buyer and the seller necessitate a pre- or post-closing possession date, it is not uncommon for the buyer to take occupancy of the home prior to the date of closing, or, in the alternative, for the seller to remain in the home for a period of time after closing.

It is recommended that a lease not be created or entered into between the buyer and the seller in effecting this early or late occupancy arrangement. If a lease agreement is used, certain landlord-tenant laws will likely come into play, and the non-occupying owner may have a more difficult time in removing the occupier if he does not vacate on a timely basis.

If an early or late occupancy agreement is entered into, a homeowner's insurance policy naming the owner as insured should be in effect during the period of occupancy by the non-owner. Also, it is wise to include a provision in the agreement that the occupier of the home is responsible for all utility charges.

The party who is occupying the home without ownership should specifically agree to pay all costs necessary to restore the premises to the condition they were in at the time of possession. Often, the occupier is required to provide a security deposit that will be held by the owner of the home during the period of occupancy to provide economic assurance for this contingency.

An agreement regarding early occupancy by a potential buyer should be executed after the purchase agreement is signed. This agreement should be a separate and distinct document, and not included in the purchase agreement itself. (There is an example of such an agreement in the Appendix.) An agreement regarding the post-closing occupancy of the home by the seller should be executed at the time of closing.

When the buyer obtains title to the home at closing, any early occupancy agreement previously allowing the buyer pre-closing possession will be automatically rendered null and void since the buyer is now the owner.

DEFAULT AND FORECLOSURE

Most homeowners do not own their homes free and clear. Rather, a security interest in the form of a mortgage or deed of trust is in place to secure the home loan. This section discusses the consequences of defaulting on the loan.

Mortgage Foreclosure

One of the most feared terms to a homeowner who is having trouble making his home loan payments is *foreclosure*. A foreclosure action is a specific type of lawsuit or legal proceeding that is brought by the lender to enforce its security interest. It usually culminates with a sale of the home to recover the money that is owed.

There must be some type of default or nonperformance on behalf of the homeowner under the terms of the mortgage and promissory note before the lender can commence with a foreclosure action. Most mortgages and notes contain a provision that if one payment is missed, the entire remaining balance becomes due and owing. This is known as an *acceleration clause* and will be discussed shortly. However, most mortgage companies go through a series of late demands, notices, and collection procedures before proceeding with the foreclosure lawsuit.

Recognize that nonpayment on the mortgage loan is not the only reason that a lender may foreclose. Generally, the homeowner must keep the property in good condition, keep satisfactory hazard insurance in place, and make timely payments on owed real estate taxes. A failure to fulfill any of these obligations by the homeowner usually prompts the lender to threaten or proceed with foreclosure.

The aforementioned acceleration clause in the mortgage and note gives the lender an absolute right to declare the entire amount of the debt due when a default has occurred. Upon default, a *notice of default* is generally forwarded to the homeowner, giving him a certain period of time to cure the default so as to avoid foreclosure. Even though the lender may not immediately notify the homeowner that a default has occurred, this does not waive its right to accelerate the amount of the debt at a later time if the payments are not made current.

If the foreclosure action is commenced, a summons must be served upon the homeowner advising him of the lawsuit. The homeowner or his attorney can usually delay the foreclosure action by filing certain pleadings with the court, but if the mortgage is valid and the default has in fact occurred, it is only a matter of time before the foreclosure action runs its course and a court order or foreclosure decree is entered. The final step in a mortgage foreclosure proceeding is to have the local sheriff or court authority sell the home so as to allow the lender to recover any remaining balance due on the mortgage loan.

Mortgage foreclosure actions are strictly regulated, and the attendant court procedures vary somewhat from state to state. Lenders usually do not favor foreclosures because they entail paying attorney fees and court costs. Although these costs can eventually be passed on to the homeowner in the form of a judgment, the initial cost must be borne by the lender.

Many states provide for some type of *stay of redemption* provision. This means that the homeowner, even after the foreclosure decree is entered, can apply to the court for several months' worth of time in an attempt to procure the necessary funds to make up all back payments. This extra opportunity for the homeowner to bring the loan current is based upon public policy that the homeowner should be given every possible chance to keep from losing his home.

Another possible result of a foreclosure action is a *deficiency balance*. If, for instance, the homeowner owes $60,000 on the mortgage loan at the time the foreclosure action commences, and the sheriff's sale of the home only results in a sale price of $55,000, the lender can obtain a *deficiency balance judgment* against the homeowner for $5,000. This $5,000 deficiency balance judgment allows the lender to try to collect the remaining $5,000 from the homeowner by traditional means of judgment collection, including garnishment of wages or bank accounts, or levies on personal property.

If the homeowner has very little equity in the home at the time of foreclosure, the homeowner may offer to voluntarily transfer his interest in the property back to the lender in exchange for a waiver of any deficiency balance that the lender would otherwise procure. This is called a *deed in lieu of foreclosure*. This, of course, would only be beneficial to the homeowner if in fact a deficiency balance judgment would be likely. Lenders sometimes agree to these offers to avoid the costs and possible delays that often accompany a foreclosure lawsuit.

Deed of Trust or Power of Sale Foreclosures

Because of the fact that mortgage foreclosures can take several months or even a year or more to effectuate, and require that the mortgage company file suit and incur legal fees and court costs, deeds of trust have become more popular with lenders.

You will recall that in a deed of trust situation, the homeowner is in essence transferring the deed to the home to a third party called a trustee. The trustee holds the deed in trust during the life of the loan. If the lender advises the trustee that the payments are not being made by the homeowner, or the homeowner is otherwise in violation of the loan agreement, the trustee proceeds with the sale of the home. Of course, various procedural and notice requirements must be given to the homeowner, including an ample opportunity to correct any alleged default, before the sale can occur.

If the homeowner is not successful in bringing his loan current or otherwise correcting the default, the trustee can proceed with selling the home without any type of lawsuit or court intervention. Only the statutory procedural requirements involved in that particular jurisdiction with regard to the enforcement of a deed of trust need be met. These usually entail a thirty- or sixty-day waiting period or opportunity to cure the default before the power of sale can be used by the trustee.

In the eyes of a lender, then, enforcement of a deed of trust is definitely the more efficient procedure to enforce its security interest on the home loan.

Land Installment Sales Contract

Remember that in a land installment sales contract it is the seller who is in essence financing the sale. The buyer makes periodic payments to the seller over an extended period of time, usually several years or more. If the buyer stops making those payments, or is otherwise in default of the contract by not maintaining the property, paying taxes on it, and the like, the seller needs to start a formal legal proceeding to protect his interests under the term of the contract.

Generally, the potential remedies available to a land contract seller are specifically provided for in the contract itself. These usually give the seller an immediate right to proceed with a breach of contract action, or an eviction action removing the buyer from the home, based upon the default. The seller has the right to obtain a judgment lien for damages if the condition of the home necessitates extensive repair.

If a buyer under a land installment sales contract has made periodic payments for several years, and then for whatever reason falls into default, it may become more difficult for the seller to obtain a court order or judgment removing the buyer from the home. In effect, the longer into the land contract, the more difficult it is to remove the buyer. This is true because courts often rule that the buyer, by making payments for an extended period of time, has obtained an *equitable interest* in the home and should not be removed without being afforded every opportunity to correct the default prior to entering the judgment or court order in favor of the seller. A carefully drafted land installment contract, granting the seller specific and definite rights, can be an advantage in the event the buyer falls into default during the term of the contract.

CONDOMINIUMS, COOPERATIVES, AND TIME-SHARING

A condominium is the ownership of a home through a deed to one particular unit in a multiple unit structure. On the surface, the owner of a condominium appears to be a tenant. The owner of the condominium unit usually also has an ownership interest in the land or other common use elements within the building or structure itself. Condominiums are sometimes also called townhomes.

The purchase of a condominium or townhome entails many of the same documents and requirements used in a typical home purchase: a purchase agreement, obtaining the necessary financing, a title search and evidence of title, and a closing.

The *common elements* of a condominium are the tenancy in common ownership interest by all the condominium owners in the common usage areas of the structure, such as hallways, elevators, recreational facilities, land, and stairwells.

The buyer of an individual condominium unit generally has to comply with a specific set of rules, called *by-laws*, that the condominium association has created. The condominium association is considered the governing body of the particular building in which the condominiums are located; it enforces these by-laws.

By-laws typically deal with the internal operation of the condominium association. The condominium association creates, enforces, and modifies these by-laws as it deems appropriate, in the best interests of the condominium owners. Further, certain condominium assessments or fees are required to be paid by the condominium owners to make sure that the aforementioned common elements of the condominium are maintained and kept in good repair.

A cooperative (also known as a co-op) is a type of home ownership in which the land and buildings are owned by one corporation. Of that corporation, the individual residents of the cooperative own stock in the corporation. These individual residents also have a lease to the specific unit in which they reside. There is no deed to the unit in which they live. The ownership of the cooperative stems from the ownership of the stock in the corporation that owns the cooperative. It is the homeowners' lease, combined with their respective stock ownership in the corporation, that creates the home ownership rights of the cooperative homeowner.

Since each cooperative homeowner owns a certain portion of the corporation's stock, it is the shareholders of the corporation who decide how the cooperative is to be run. In essence, the homeowner in the cooperative is the tenant as well as the landlord.

Purchasing of a cooperative by an individual is different than the typical home purchase in the sense that no deed to any type of real estate interest is involved. Rather, the only financing necessary is for the cooperative owner to purchase the stock in the cooperative corporation. Once that occurs, the lease agreement is entered into and the periodic payments pursuant to the terms of the lease from the cooperative owner to the cooperative corporation are made. Generally, cooperative corporations are fairly strict and exclusive in deciding whom they allow to purchase stock and enter into a lease agreement in their cooperative.

Time-sharing is a situation in which many individuals own separate, undivided interests in a piece of property and the right to occupy the property only during a specific pre-determined period of time.

Time-shares are most often used by people purchasing an interest in a vacation home so as to utilize the premises as a resort locale rather than a residence. The purchase of a time-share is accomplished by written contract. Due to the aforementioned use restrictions, re-sale of time-share property can sometimes prove difficult.

FAIR HOUSING LAWS

In 1968, the federal government passed a body of laws termed the Fair Housing Act. In essence, these laws prohibit discrimination on the sale of residential real estate based on race, color, religion, national origin, and, in a later amendment, sex. Under this Act, residential property is defined as any building occupied or designed to be occupied as a residence, including vacant lands sold for the construction of a home.

The Fair Housing Act of 1968 makes the following activities illegal:

1. The refusal to sell, rent, or negotiate with any individual or otherwise make a dwelling unavailable to any individual based upon race, color, religion, national origin, and sex.
2. Changing the terms, conditions, or services offered for the purchase, sale, or lease of a residence based upon the aforementioned classification as a means of discrimination.
3. Discriminating through any statement or advertisement that restricts the sale or rental of residential property based upon any of the aforementioned classifications.
4. Indicating to any individual of the aforementioned classifications that a particular dwelling is not available for sale or lease solely on the basis of that individual's classification.
5. Attempting to make a profit by persuading homeowners to sell or lease their homes because of the possible entry into their neighborhood of persons of a particular race, color, religion, or national origin.
6. Changing the terms, conditions, or requirements for a home loan to any individual who wishes to purchase a home, or otherwise denying such a loan on the basis of the aforementioned classifications.
7. The demotion or discharging of any employee or agent, or reducing compensation of an employee or agent because they have otherwise complied with the nondiscrimination sections of the Fair Housing Act.
8. Threatening, interfering, coercing, or intimidating any individual who is otherwise exercising and enjoying the rights granted under the Fair Housing Act.

The Fair Housing Act does not apply to the sale or rental of commercial or industrial properties. Further, an individual may discriminate on the basis of any of the aforementioned classifications and not be in violation of the Fair Housing Act if he can meet the following criteria:

1. He does not own any more than three homes at any one time.
2. The seller is living in the home or was the last person to live in the home being sold (if this residency requirement is not met, then the exception applies to only one sale every two years).
3. The seller cannot involve or utilize a real estate broker to facilitate or cause the sale to be made.
4. The seller must not use any type of discriminatory advertising in selling or attempting to sell the home.

The Fair Housing Act also states that a residence owned by a religious sect or organization does not have to sell that residence to an individual not a member of the sect or organization, provided that the potential buyer is not prohibited from joining said religious organization. Also, the religious organization owning the property cannot be based upon one of the previously mentioned classifications.

LEASE WITH OPTION TO PURCHASE

Sometimes when a homeowner is having a difficult time in selling, he will agree to allow a potential buyer to lease the property, which includes an option to purchase. Options to purchase (without a lease) were referred to in Chapter 2.

A buyer who is leasing a home will enter into a written lease for a specified monthly payment, which will generally equate to the seller's existing mortgage payment, including property taxes and insurance. This allows the seller to, in essence, pass through the rent payment to his mortgage company so he is not losing any money while the house would otherwise sit vacant.

The tenant also executes an option to purchase if he is interested in purchasing the home. The typical arrangement provides for all rental monies to be credited toward the eventual purchase price of the home if the option is exercised. This, of course, gives the tenant added incentive to become a buyer as he (if the decision is made not to buy) relinquishes his right to have all prior rent payments applied to the purchase price of the home.

Sellers who enter into a lease with an option to purchase are in effect taking their home off the market with regard to other potential buyers. This is obviously a factor that needs to be considered by the homeowner before entering into this type of arrangement.

If the option to purchase already includes the specific agreed upon purchase price, and during the rental period the market value of the home is reduced, the renter will have less incentive to exercise the option. Of course, the purchase price can always be renegotiated.

The seller should check with his mortgage lender before entering into a lease with an option to purchase. The lender needs to be made aware that the agreement is not a sale, so that it does not effectuate the due on sale clause requiring the seller to pay off the balance of the loan prior to the home being sold and the funds becoming available.

6

New Home Construction and Major Remodeling Projects

Building a new home or undertaking a major remodeling project can be either one of the most satisfying or one of the most frustrating experiences of a homeowner. The "marriage" between the homeowner and the builder during the project can be either strained, difficult, and disappointing or delightful, creative, and economically beneficial. Often what starts out to be a mutually acceptable arrangement ends up being resolved in court. The purpose of this chapter is to review the legal aspects of such a project, including dealing with a home builder or remodeling contractor.

THE HOME BUILDER OR GENERAL CONTRACTOR

Individual, Partnership, or Corporation

Before entering into any type of contract concerning home construction, the homeowner or buyer must determine whether he is dealing with an individual, a partnership, or a corporation. That is, when it comes time to enter into the contract, if the home builder's name on the contract is Jones Home Construction and the signature of the builder is Bill Jones, the question arises, is Jones Home Construction a corporation or an individual? If something should go wrong during the construction process, who is the responsible party?

The homeowner should always inquire and satisfy himself that he is dealing with an individual, a partnership or a corporation. And, as such, all documentation that is executed should either be signed by the individual or by an authorized representative of the partnership or corporation, such as a corporate officer or general partner.

Business Check

If the homeowner has entered into a contract with a corporate builder, he should contact the Secretary of State's office to determine that the corporation is in current good standing. However, this is only indicative of whether the corporation is conducting its internal affairs according to the law and is no guarantee that the corporation is solvent or does quality work.

The homeowner can contact local or state licensing boards to determine whether the builder is registered as a member of the various local trade building boards. Although this is also no guarantee of the quality or type of individual or company the homeowner is dealing with, if the builder is not listed with these licensing boards or is not a corporation recognized by the Secretary of State, further inquiries need to be made.

An added step that the homeowner can take prior to entering into the home construction or remodeling contract is to check with the local clerk of the court to discover if there are any civil judgments or pending lawsuits against the builder. This will allow the homeowner to determine whether the builder has been sued in the past and, if so, if the lawsuit was brought by a disgruntled homeowner as a result of alleged improper work. Any type of lawsuit in this regard should put the homeowner on his guard prior to entering into the contract.

It is also a good idea for the homeowner to check with the local federal bankruptcy court to determine whether the individual or corporate builder has ever filed bankruptcy. Obviously, if this is the case, the builder's economic stability and/or financial management are in question. If the builder is currently in bankruptcy, any contract entered into by the homeowner with the builder could possibly be voided or limited in effect by the bankruptcy court or the bankruptcy trustee, depending upon the type of bankruptcy filed and the current status of the bankruptcy proceedings.

The Bid Process There is no strict legal mechanism to determine which particular builder will provide the best product for the best price. Word of mouth, references, and the like are all factors that the homeowner must weigh prior to entering into a contract. These considerations, coupled with the business check particulars mentioned in the previous section, should give the homeowner enough background information to allow for an intelligent and reasonable decision. It is generally recommended that at least three prospective builders be interviewed and researched before entering into any type of contract for the work involved, especially if the project is the construction of a new home.

THE CONTRACT Since the construction of a new home or major remodeling project almost always entails a large sum of money, the contract should be as specific as the homeowner and the builder will allow. General and vague terms within the contract can only lead to problems. Vague terminology can always be interpreted different ways and will make it difficult to enforce the contract if a dispute should arise later.

This section reviews all essential and recommended optional provisions in a contract for new home construction and major remodeling projects. Some of the particular topics covered may only pertain to either new home construction or remodeling projects.

Parties The name of the builder, and whether the builder is an individual, a partnership, or a corporation, should be stated clearly in the contract. If the builder is a corporation, the individual signing on behalf of the corporation should indicate his capacity to sign. That is, he should indicate that he is either the president, the vice president, or some corporate officer. The homeowner should also sign the agreement.

Both parties should include their current addresses in the event that written notification to one another is required during the term of the contract. If the home is owned by more than one individual, all owners should sign the contract so as to avoid any future problems with regard to authorization of the work.

Work Description   It should be stated in a general way that the builder is to build the home or make the improvements agreed upon pursuant to specifically agreed upon plans and specifications approved by the parties. These plans and specifications, although not necessarily contained in the contract, should be referred to as part of the contract and can be attached as an exhibit.

Often the contract refers to working drawings and specifications as two separate items. The working drawings are a layman-oriented design of the components involved in the work to be done. They can include a rudimentary blueprint and are usually drawn to scale.

When the contract refers to the specifications or specs of the plans, it is referring to the technical details with regard to the equipment, construction methods, and the like. The specifications usually take precedent over working drawings.

Generally, the more detailed the information is regarding work description, the less flexibility the builder will have in completing the job. The goal is to leave as little as possible to chance or subsequent interpretation by either the builder or the homeowner, so that no disputes concerning what exactly needs to be done will arise. If the homeowner is not comfortable with or does not understand the specifications or working drawings that are referred to in the contract, further questions and inquiries need to be made before signing.

If an architect is being used in the construction project, it is the architect's duty to make sure that the working drawings and specifications coincide with what the homeowner has contracted the architect to provide. In this sense, the homeowner has delegated the review of the work specifications to the architect and made him responsible for seeing that the work contracted for is what the architect has drafted.

There should be a statement in the contract that all materials, labor, and fees necessary to complete construction of the home or home improvement are furnished by the builder. Also, a clause that all work and labor performed by the builder is to be done in a standard workmanlike manner is desirable.

There should also be a statement in the contract that the builder or architect will be responsible for compliance with all local restrictive covenants concerning the design of the home or home improvement. Certain areas have enforceable covenants (private building codes) that require all construction or home improvements to be approved by a homeowners' association. The burden of making sure that the construction is in accordance with all such local covenants should be passed on to the builder or architect. The legal description and street address of the home being built or worked on should also be included in the contract.

A provision stating that the builder is an *independent contractor* and not an employee of the homeowner is to be included in the contract. By not being considered an employee of the homeowner, certain liabilities that may be incurred by the builder cannot be passed on to the homeowner. In any event, a statement to this independent contractor status serves to clarify the parties' position to one another so as to ensure that the homeowner is not held liable for any injuries or damages arising from the negligence of the builder, or anyone in his employment, during the term of the contract.

Schedule of Work Although most dates referred to in a contract of this type are target dates, due to various factors beyond the homeowner's and builder's control, specific dates should nevertheless be mentioned in the contract so as to provide as much specificity as possible regarding when the work is to begin and end. The homeowner would be wise to insist that a clause in the contract exist, stating that the work is to begin on a certain date and, if that date is not met within a certain specified period thereafter (such as twenty days), then a material breach of the contract has occurred and the homeowner may elect to declare the contract null and void. This gives the homeowner leverage to see that the builder commences the work on a timely basis.

A scheduled date of completion should also be contained in the contract. A statement that it is the builder's responsibility to see that all normal and workmanlike progress in the project is met, in keeping with sound construction practices, further gives the homeowner a contractual legal advantage in the event that the project appears to be delayed unnecessarily or without good reason.

Most major home improvement contracts or contracts for the purchase of a new home contain a phrase to protect the builder as follows:

> If any type of labor dispute, labor strike, or unavailability of material exists during the term of this contract, the contractor will not in any way be held legally responsible for said interruption, delay, or the like.

This particular clause is merely a reflection of the reality of the construction business that certain aspects of the project are outside the control of the builder. Further, most builders will include in the contract a provision that weather-related delays will not be cause for termination of the contract by the homeowner.

Payment The total cost of the project should be stated in the contract. Whether a new home construction or a major home improvement, some type of payment schedule should be incorporated within the contract.

All payments from the homeowner to the builder should be staggered in nature. That is, the work should be paid for as it is completed. By paying in advance, the homeowner loses any leverage he has in requiring the builder to finish the project.

Usually the payment from the homeowner to the contractor making an improvement on an existing home is between 25 and 50 percent upon commencement of the project and the balance to be paid upon completion.

With regard to new home construction, generally four or five equal payments are involved, with the last payment to the builder being made at the time of completion. The other payments can be made as follows: first payment, when the foundation is complete; second payment, when all plumbing and mechanical aspects of the home are done; third payment, when the finish carpentry and cabinetry are completed; and the final payment when the home is totally constructed and a *certificate of occupancy* is granted by the local authorities.

In the case of new home construction, it should be stated in the contract that the homeowner is to receive five to ten days' written notice from the builder before a payment is due. This gives the homeowner ample opportunity to procure the funds from his lender.

Role and Payment of Subcontractors

In most major construction projects, the builder hires subcontractors to do various aspects of the work. The subcontractors are to be paid by the builder. Subcontractors do have the right to file liens against the homeowner's property if they are not paid. Hence, the homeowner does not want to run the risk of paying a builder without seeing that the subcontractors are also paid.

There are different avenues for accomplishing this. First, a general provision can be included in the contract stating that the builder will sign a general lien waiver upon each payment from the homeowner, to cover all invoices and amounts due on the job to date. Then, at the time of final occupancy, the builder must provide the homeowner with a lien waiver guaranteeing that all materials and labor to date are paid for in full, and that no liens or potential liens can be filed against the homeowner's property.

With regard to major home remodeling projects, the homeowner can pay all subcontractors or suppliers directly, to make sure that they do not retain any rights to file a lien against the home for nonpayment.

Permits, Zoning, and Licenses

It should be stated in the contract that the builder is to procure all necessary permits and licenses, to satisfy zoning requirements, and to do the construction work. A blanket statement to the effect that the builder shall obtain the necessary permits from all proper authorities for the work contracted for usually suffices.

Another provision that would further protect the legal rights of the homeowner would be that the builder shall keep the homeowner *indemnified* from any fines or losses incurred by reason of the builder not abiding by the aforementioned provision. This means that if any fine is levied against the homeowner for failure to obtain any required permit, the homeowner has a cause of action against the builder for that amount. A clause in the contract stating that all building code rules and regulations are to be complied with by the builder is another method of protecting the homeowner in this regard.

Modifications and Change Orders A clause in the contract that allows the homeowner to request changes in the work to be done without causing the contract to be invalid should also be included. Any substantive change orders need to be made in writing by the homeowner to the builder. The builder will always reserve the right in the contract to increase the cost of the project in accord with the requested change order.

A homeowner should never enter into a contract that does not allow for a change order provision. As long as the homeowner is willing to pay any reasonable charge for a particular change in the work to be done during the term of a contract, there is no need to preclude this option. Remember that a change order usually takes the form of an addendum to the original contract and, as such, needs to be in writing to avoid confusion as to what is required by the contract and the agreed upon changes. Oral modifications of written contracts often lead to disputes and are difficult to enforce.

Builder Liability The contract should require the builder at all times during the progress of the work to keep the project insured from loss or damage by fire, lightning, tornado, or other types of natural casualties. The contract should also state that any type of theft or vandalism on the project shall be the builder's responsibility, including all materials delivered to the project site that have not yet been incorporated in the construction.

Another necessary provision to the contract is that the builder is to be responsible for and provide necessary worker's compensation and liability insurance for any workers, employees, subcontractors, and suppliers. Since the property will most likely be in the homeowner's name during the period of construction, any injured party can legally name the homeowner as a co-defendant to a lawsuit along with the builder. If the builder has this type of insurance in place, it will be his insurance company that provides required legal defense or any necessary compensation to the injured party.

Performance Bond The homeowner will sometimes insist that a bond be provided by the builder that insures completion of the work if the builder fails to do so. Generally, the bonding company will reimburse the homeowner for any extra cost in completing the work that was to be done under the terms of the contract. Recognize, however, that the inclusion of this provision in the contract and its cost to the builder are usually passed on to the homeowner. Even so, it is recommended that a bond requirement be placed in the contract for large projects or anytime the homeowner wants to make sure that all precautions are taken to protect his interests.

Completing the Project There should always be some type of clause in the contract stating that the builder will remove all remaining materials and unused items from the job site when the project is completed.

On a related note, if weather conditions do not allow the completion of certain exterior items such as sod, grading, outside painting, or concrete work, the homeowner will often be allowed to take possession of the otherwise substantially completed residence and put into escrow (held by a third party) the amount of money necessary to complete the work. The escrowed money will be released to the builder when the work is completed. Generally, an amount 1½ times the anticipated cost of the work to be completed is escrowed. This allows the homeowner to actually take possession of the home prior to completion, if he so desires. It is good idea to include a clause in the contract giving the homeowner this option.

Three-Day Right of Recision Under federal law, any homeowner entering into a home improvement contract that may result in a lien or other security interest being filed on the home has, without any penalty or obligation, three business days from the date of the contract to cancel the transaction. The homeowner is entitled to receive a refund for any down payment if the contract is canceled. This gives the homeowner an additional method of releasing himself from any contractual obligation.

If the homeowner does decide to cancel the contract pursuant to this law, personal or written notice needs to be forwarded to the builder. The homeowner needs to be able to prove that this notice was given within three days of the date of the contract. Personal delivery or certified mail, return receipt requested, is the best way to ensure this.

Form Agreements When an individual is in the process of entering into an agreement for new home construction or a major home improvement, the builder usually has a pre-printed form or standard agreement that he has used in the past. There is nothing inherently wrong with using a form agreement, as long as all the necessary terms are included.

If, for whatever reason, the contract proposed by the builder is not acceptable, either a new contract can be drafted or an addendum specifying any changes or additions to the original contract can be signed.

Financing Contingency If the homeowner must obtain a loan to allow him to pay for the work or new construction, a contingency in the contract must be drafted to reflect this. It will have to be noted in the contract that the agreement and respective duties and obligations of the parties will not be binding if the necessary funds are not procured by the homeowner, at an acceptable rate of interest or term of repayment.

Warranties In the past, most homeowners undertaking major construction projects or having a home built were totally at risk. The concept of *caveat* *emptor* (meaning "buyer beware") was the rule. However, in the last fifteen to twenty years, expressed and implied warranties have come into play.

Initially, an *implied warranty* meant that the courts will rule that a certain product or service must meet reasonable standards of construction and competency. Even though no written warranty may be given, the builder may be held liable for breach of warranty if the product he delivers is substantially below generally accepted standards. The homeowner should never rely on an implied warranty but should always obtain an expressed written warranty, which would be included in the contract.

With regard to new construction, most competent builders will warrant all workmanship, labor, and material for a period of at least one calendar year from the date of occupancy, in addition to any manufacturers' warranties, which may extend beyond that time frame with regard to products utilized in the home.

Some new home builders offer a warranty that has been developed by the National Association of Home Builders, called the Home Owners' Warranty, or HOW. Generally, this provides warranty protection against certain major structural defects up to ten years. It requires the builder to complete or correct any type of defect caused by faulty workmanship or materials due to non-compliance with HOW standards during the initial year after construction.

During the second year, the builder's warranty continues to protect against any defects in the electrical, plumbing, and heating and cooling systems of the home, and against any major structural defects. For years three through ten, a national insurance plan directly insures the home buyer against structural defects.

If a dispute arises over the scope of HOW coverage, and the dispute cannot be settled by the builder and the buyer, the issue is referred to a regional HOW agency, which will appoint a person or committee to try to resolve the differences. If that does not resolve the dispute, an arbitration hearing will occur.

If a homeowner desires a HOW warranty, a fee is charged and added onto the construction price, usually amounting to a certain amount per thousand dollars of the construction cost. The cost of the HOW warranty will be paid by the builder, although it will be passed on to the homeowner in the total purchase price. The HOW warranty, if obtained, can be transferred to a subsequent buyer if the aforementioned ten-year period is still in effect when the home is sold.

Arbitration To save a costly court battle in the event that a dispute arises pursuant to the terms or implications of the contract, many contracts contain a provision that calls for the parties to resolve their dispute by arbitration. Arbitration is a quick and relatively inexpensive process in which a designated third party arbitration panel or individual hears each side's arguments and decides any respective liability or fault.

Although an arbitration provision may be contained in a contract, in many states the parties to the contract nevertheless retain their right to proceed with formal legal action subsequent to arbitration if they so choose.

FINANCING THE PROJECT

New Home Construction Loans

When a new home is being purchased and constructed, the contract entered into between the buyer and the builder will usually be a hybrid of two separate contracts: a standard real estate purchase agreement for the purchase of a home (as discussed in Chapter 2) and a new construction contract as discussed here. Often the main contingency in the standard purchase contract is whether the buyer can obtain a loan to finance the construction. Under certain circumstances, the builder may agree to finance the home's construction, and the buyer will be obligated to purchase the home upon completion.

In most other cases, however, it is the homeowner who has to obtain a commitment for the necessary funds to pay for the completed home prior to the builder proceeding with construction. The lender usually does the prerequisite background credit check on the buyer, as done in any type of real estate loan, and often works directly with the builder once the loan has been approved as to payments on the project.

Recall that since the lender will be obtaining a mortgage or security interest in the completed home in exchange for the loan proceeds, it is in the lender's interest to make sure that no other liens or potential liens are filed on the property. This obviously works also to protect the buyer's interest.

In this regard, then, the lender will typically only forward the necessary construction funds to the builder when written evidence is provided that all subcontractors and suppliers have been paid. This evidence includes written lien waivers or paid invoices.

Home Improvement Loan

A home improvement loan is money being lent for a specified improvement. The funds are earmarked to a specific project on the existing home, and the lender will require some type of security or lien against the home in exchange for the loan. If a mortgage or security interest is placed on the home pursuant to the loan being made, any interest charged and paid will be tax deductible.

The lender will often monitor the construction and pay the contractor directly, as in a new home construction loan. However, unlike most new home construction loans, which can be mortgaged for thirty years, most home improvement loans range from only five to ten years in length, with the interest rate charged being somewhat higher than that for a typical first mortgage loan.

Home Equity Credit Line

Another method of financing a major home improvement is a home equity line of credit. The homeowner receives a certain loan amount, which can be drawn upon from the lender as needed. Depending upon the amount of money borrowed in a particular time, the repayment schedule is modified accordingly.

Any interest paid is tax deductible, and the interest rate charged is usually adjustable, depending upon the prevailing rates when the line of credit is utilized. There often is an initial charge for establishing this type of equitable line of credit, but the interest rate is somewhat less than that charged for a home improvement loan.

Second Mortgage

Second mortgages are used in remodeling projects costing a substantial sum of money. The interest rate on a second mortgage may be lower than in the other loan options already mentioned.

When applying for a second mortgage, certain initial costs such as credit checks, appraisal fees, and title insurance are involved. The mortgage payback period can range from five to fifteen years, depending upon the interest rate being charged and what the lender is willing to offer.

DEFAULT BY CONTRACTOR

No matter how tightly, concisely, or legally precise a contract may be, problems can still arise. In the worst case scenario, the builder fails to fulfill his obligations under the terms of the contract and leaves the homeowner with no option but to proceed with a lawsuit. This section reviews the various types of conduct that rise to the level of a breach of contract by a builder.

Uncompleted Work or Slow Completion

As previously mentioned, the contract for new home construction or a major home improvement should always state a certain starting date and an anticipated completion date for the project. Although there are certain instances in which the work cannot be completed due to factors outside the builder's control (such as weather or lack of available materials), any prolonged interruption of construction is justifiable grounds for declaring the builder to be in breach of the contract. In this case, the homeowner or his attorney should notify the builder that the homeowner considers the contract breached and terminate the relationship with the builder while reserving the right to hold him legally responsible for all resulting damages and expenses.

Quality of Workmanship

As already stated, the contract should contain some type of general statement concerning the expected quality of workmanship. If the quality of the work is so inherently poor prior to completion, the homeowner may decide not to allow the builder to complete the project and notify him to cease with all further work. The homeowner should always obtain a third party opinion with regard to the qualitative deficiency in the workmanship before taking this step, preferably by someone in the construction industry.

Other Reasons for Default

If the builder fails to comply with any building codes or does not obtain the necessary permits for the construction involved, this constitutes justifiable grounds for terminating the contract on behalf of the homeowner. As mentioned, this requirement should be put in the contract, although it has been held by some courts that this is implied in the contract by hiring a professional builder to do the work.

Also, regardless of the stage of the contract or the type of work being done, the death of the builder also terminates the contract and the builder's obligations under the contract. Any money owed the builder at that time should be paid to the builder's estate or legal heirs. The filing of bankruptcy or evidence that the builder is out of business is also legal grounds for the homeowner to declare the contract null and void.

Remedies Anytime a homeowner believes that the builder is not performing pursuant to the terms of the contract, the first thing to do is consult an attorney. The homeowner is usually too close to the problem to see objectively the legal ramifications of what, if anything, the builder is doing incorrectly. The attorney can usually give sufficient advice and direction to the homeowner as to whether a breach has occurred and, if so, which remedy to pursue.

Depending upon the amount of money involved, the homeowner may wish to pursue formal legal action. There are two directions to take in this regard. One is called *specific performance*. This requires the builder to complete the job pursuant to the terms of the contract. If for whatever reason the builder has not completed the job, or failed to complete the job pursuant to the terms of the contract, it is doubtful that the homeowner will want to obtain a court order requiring the builder to complete the work, since presumably all faith in the builder is gone. Nevertheless, the remedy of specific performance is an option.

If a breach by the builder has occurred, the homeowner will usually have the work completed by another builder and then file suit against the original builder for any damages or extra costs incurred because of the breach.

Always keep in mind that the damaged homeowner does have a duty to mitigate his damages. Simply put, this means that the homeowner must do everything possible to minimize his losses. If the homeowner has done everything possible to reduce his damages and still suffers enough of a loss to warrant a lawsuit, he must decide whether hiring an attorney and proceeding with legal action will prove cost beneficial.

Another option available to the homeowner is to file suit in the local small claims or people's court. These types of courts have a limited jurisdiction of several hundred to several thousand dollars. However, no attorneys are required, and decisions are typically made by the court within a relatively short period of time.

7

Taxes

It was stated at the beginning of this book that the information contained herein is not to be taken as specific advice, due to the variance in local laws and their applicability to different circumstances. Nowhere is this disclaimer more applicable than this chapter on taxes and the home.

Not only are the tax laws constantly being updated and revised, but court decisions and tax rulings are continually changing the standards and prerequisites necessary to gain a tax advantage. Always check with a qualified tax accountant or tax attorney prior to making any decision with regard to your home on the basis of possible tax ramifications.

DEDUCTIONS

This section deals with deductions on a tax return; that is, amounts that can be subtracted from an individual's or a couple's adjusted gross income so as to reduce their tax liability.

Property Taxes

With some limited exceptions, all homeowners pay property taxes. Usually, the amount of the tax depends upon the assessed value of the home.

Property taxes on your residence are deductible. Even if the owner is paying his property taxes to the lender in an escrow account, and the lender in turn pays the property taxes on your behalf, the owner is entitled to the tax deductibility on the taxes paid. The lender sends an annual statement to the owner indicating the amount paid for property taxes during the calendar year. If a lender is not involved, the local tax assessor's office provides this information.

Mortgage Interest Payments

As with property taxes, any interest that a homeowner pays to the lender on a mortgage, deed of trust, or land installment sales contract is deductible from the owner's adjusted gross income when determining income tax liability. The lender or seller must send the owner a statement indicating the amount of interest paid on the loan or purchase contract during the preceding calendar year.

This interest deductibility is especially advantageous to homeowners who are in the early years of their loan. This is so because the bulk of the monthly principal and interest payment to the lender is, in fact, interest. As the years go by and payments on the loan are made, more principal will be paid than interest, thus reducing the tax advantage of the monthly loan payment.

Other Types of Interest Deductions

Also deductible from the homeowner's adjusted gross income is all interest paid on any loan secured by a second mortgage or deed of trust. This interest is totally deductible, just as if the interest were paid on a loan secured by a first mortgage or deed of trust, regardless of what the loan funds are used for.

When a homeowner procures a home improvement loan that is secured by the property being improved, the interest paid pursuant to the loan is also deductible. The lender must obtain some type of mortgage, deed of trust, or other security in the home before the interest can be deducted.

Interest paid by the homeowner on a home equity line of credit can be deducted from the homeowner's adjusted gross income. Keep in mind, however, that there is no tax advantage to obtaining a home equity loan unless the homeowner itemizes his deductions. Currently, the interest on a home equity loan or a home equity line of credit is one hundred percent deductible if the loan is $100,000 or less. Above that amount, the interest deductibility is reduced.

Taxes on Utility Payments

In some jurisdictions, certain electric and natural gas utility bills include a tax that is the same rate as a local or state sales tax. Payment of this type of utility tax is deductible.

Medical Home Improvements

Home improvements for medical reasons can be tax deductible if specifically prescribed by a physician. Examples of such a medically required home improvement would be an in-house elevator (as opposed to stairs) for someone with a severe heart condition, or ramps instead of stairs on the entrance to the home of a person who has been confined to a wheelchair.

Energy-Saving Home Improvements

Certain home improvements designed to conserve and use energy efficiently may be eligible for federal tax credits. Although not deductible, the tax credit is subtracted from any income tax liability.

The types of improvements that may qualify for an energy conservation federal tax credit include certain types of insulation, thermal doors and windows, weather stripping and caulking on the exterior of the home, automatic thermostatic control, and others.

Certain states also provide for tax credit or tax incentives for installing energy-saving devices, such as solar panels, wind and geothermal energy devices, and similar types of energy-saving improvements.

The homeowner should check with his state's department of revenue to determine what qualifies for a tax break regarding energy-saving improvements in that area.

Losses Attributable to Theft   Generally, in the absence of applicable insurance coverage that reimburses the homeowner, a deduction can be had from any loss stemming from theft. The homeowner is required to prove to the satisfaction of the Internal Revenue Service that a theft has occurred that resulted in the loss of the personal property, as opposed to merely misplacing the items involved. Also, the homeowner must be able to document to the Internal Revenue's satisfaction the value of the property that was stolen.

Casualty Losses   If some type of natural disaster should strike, and the homeowner incurs not only damage to the home but also damage to the personal property within the home, part of the loss may be tax deductible. Of course, this does not include any type of loss that is reimbursed to the homeowner by way of insurance. As with theft losses, any casualty losses must be adequately documented with regard to the claimed value of the damaged or destroyed items.

Closing Costs   When a buyer purchases a home, several cost items of the purchase, including obtaining the loan, may be tax deductible.

Discount points of the loan, each point amounting to one percent of the loan, are deductible in the year in which they are paid. In the case of the home purchase, discount points are deductible by the buyer for the year in which the closing occurred.

Often, the seller of the home has already paid for a part of the annual real estate taxes for a period of time after the closing date. If this is the case, the buyer reimburses the seller for these previously paid property taxes at closing. The buyer should make sure that his repayment of these property taxes back to the seller is included as a deductible item on his income tax return.

Any prepaid interest by the homeowner is also deductible from his adjusted gross income. That is, any interest paid to the lender between the time of closing and the time of the initial mortgage payment is deductible.

Certain closing costs, however, are not deductible. Any type of filing fees charged by the local offices to file documents, such as deeds or security instruments, are not deductible. Any charges made by the lender for a credit check on the buyer are not deductible. Any title insurance costs are not deductible. Also, any fees paid to an attorney pursuant to the home purchase are non-deductible.

The homeowner should always make sure that on the real estate closing settlement statement the discount points charged for the loan are clearly identified as loan origination or loan discount points. Otherwise, the IRS may question whether these charges are actually discount points, or merely some type of administrative costs being charged for the loan. To constitute deductible discount points, they must be computed as a percentage of the amount borrowed. This means that the amount charged for each discount point should specifically compute out to be one percent of the total loan amount. If they do not, it is doubtful they will pass as a deductible item.

Also with regard to discount points, the IRS requires that they be paid directly to the lender from the homeowner, as opposed to simply discounting or subtracting the loan discount points from the total loan amount.

Discount points paid in connection with a home improvement loan or a vacation home loan are not generally deductible.

With regard to refinancing the loan on the home, any discount points paid are deductible, but not on a 100 percent basis at the time the loan is made. Their deductibility must be spread out over the life of the loan. Keep in mind, however, that if a homeowner is refinancing for the second time, any discount points not yet deducted on the first refinanced loan can now be deducted in full for the year in which the second refinancing has occurred.

SALE OF THE HOME

Often when a homeowner sells his home, a profit is realized. The question then becomes whether the profit realized by the homeowner is taxable income. This section discusses the ramifications of the home sale and how the tax laws come into play.

Taxable Event

The Internal Revenue Service considers the sale of a person's principal residence a taxable event. If a profit is realized by the homeowner upon the sale of his home, and certain specific exceptions do not apply, this profit is taxed as ordinary income. Usually, however, the rollover exception discussed in the next paragraph causes the tax liability to be deferred. Under current law, if the home is sold at a loss, any such loss sustained by the homeowner cannot be deducted.

Deferring of Tax on Home Sale Profit (Rollover Exception)

If a homeowner sells his home at a profit, and then buys or builds a new home within a two-year period thereafter, the entire profit realized from the previous sale will be deferred if the price of the new home is more than the *adjusted sale price* of the old home. The adjusted sale price of the homeowner's previous home can be determined by the sale price of the home minus any expenses incurred in preparing the home for sale.

This rule applies to all homeowners, regardless of age. However, keep in mind that the homeowner must purchase and occupy a new home within two years after the sale of the previous residence, and the home purchased within the two-year period of time must be your principal residence. The obvious import of this rule is that it is advantageous from a tax standpoint not only to purchase another home, but to purchase a more expensive home when selling one's current residence.

One-Time Exclusion   If a homeowner is fifty-five or older, up to $125,000 of profit from the sale of his home can be exempted from federal income tax, even if a new home is not purchased within the aforementioned two-year time period. This $125,000 exclusion can be used only once in a lifetime. Also, the homeowner must have owned and lived in the property as his principal residence for at least three of the five years prior to the sale occurring.

If a married couple holds title to their home jointly and files a joint tax return for the year of the sale of their home, and either spouse meets the fifty-five or older and principal residence use requirement, both will be able to qualify for the one-time exclusion. However, if either the husband or the wife has previously elected to take advantage of the $125,000 exclusion, it cannot be used again by either spouse while they are married. The general rule, then, is that there is one $125,000 exclusion per married couple.

Certain exceptions do apply, depending upon divorce, previous death of one of the spouses, and the like. The IRS or a local tax accountant should be consulted if the homeowner is unsure about his ability to utilize this one-time exclusion upon the sale of his home. The policy reason behind the exclusion rule is that elderly people who may possibly be on a fixed income should not be penalized late in life with a major tax liability.

Tax Effective Home Improvements   When a homeowner sells his home, the difference between what he originally paid for the home and the price the house subsequently sold for is not necessarily the taxable profit on the home. The homeowner must determine the *basis* of the home.

For tax purposes, a home's basis is anything that the homeowner was required to pay to purchase the property, including any non-deductible closing expenses. The determination of the tax basis of the home is important because it determines the amount of taxable gain on the sale, assuming another home is not purchased within two years pursuant to the tax deferral rules previously discussed.

Various restrictions and definitions apply with regard to the basis of a home. As a general rule, however, major types of additions and permanent improvements that increase the value of the home will reduce the taxable profit to the seller when the home is eventually sold. Any type of repair or maintenance expense that keeps the home in its current condition, however, is not considered a permanent home improvement and consequently cannot be used as an increase in the home's value or basis for income tax purposes when the home is sold.

Moving and Relocation Expenses   When a homeowner is forced to move his principal residence from one area to another due to a job transfer, some types of income tax deductions are allowed. Certain criteria must be met before any tax deductions will be considered. These criteria include: the homeowner must itemize his deductions; the transfer to new employment must be thirty-five or more miles farther from the homeowner's old residence than the homeowner's new residence; the homeowner has worked full-time at this particular job for thirty-nine out of the previous fifty-two weeks subsequent to the move occurring, or, in the alternative, if the individual is self-employed, he must be self-employed at this particular vocation for seventy-eight out of the previous 104 weeks.

If the prerequisites mentioned in the previous paragraph are met, the homeowner can generally deduct any reasonable cost in locating a new home. This includes travel expenses to the area where the new residence is located and eighty percent of all lodging and meal costs incurred during the search period.

Any moving costs such as packing, shipping, and insurance and storage on personal property for thirty days or less may be deductible. The cost of moving the homeowner and his family can also be deducted up to 80 percent of reasonable meal and lodging expenses. If temporary living expenses are required, the same 80 percent rule for room and board also applies, up to a maximum of thirty days subsequent to the move if a new home is not purchased or available for occupancy.

Certain costs of the sale of the homeowner's previous residence can also be deducted, including most attorney fees, real estate commissions, and any transfer taxes involved. Appraisal costs and title insurance fees may also be deductible.

There are limits on how much can be deductible for moving expenses. With regard to locating a new home and any incurred temporary living expenses, the amount is currently $1,500 (1992 figure). Any costs pertaining to purchasing or selling of the current home can be deductible only up to $3,000. Of course, if the homeowner is reimbursed by his employer for any of this type of expenses, the reimbursement is considered income, which would obviously offset the deductions otherwise allowed.

Rental Income If the homeowner is in the process of leasing out his home for a short period of time prior to selling it, such as in a situation where the prospective buyer has entered into a lease with an option to buy, the homeowner/landlord must report all rental money received as taxable income. However, much of this income can be offset by way of allowable deductible expenses.

These allowable expenses include all broker fees, management fees, advertisements, property taxes, mortgage interest payments, and any general maintenance costs and utilities that the homeowner/landlord has paid.

Keep in mind, however, that a potential tax pitfall in leasing out one's principal residence is that the aforementioned two-year deferral of any otherwise taxable gain on the sale of the home applies only when the homeowner moves from one principal residence to another. It does not apply when the homeowner sells what is otherwise considered rental property.

In this regard, then, the homeowner must be able to convince the IRS that the lease of the home is a temporary situation and not a permanent source of rental income. The homeowner's position is that he is not leasing out the home for the long-term, but as an alternative to allowing the property to sit vacant while unsold. Of course, a duly executed lease with option to purchase by the current tenant would add clout to the homeowner's position in this regard.

THE SECOND HOME

Deductions on a homeowner's second home or vacation home are available. Certain expenses, such as real estate taxes and interest on the home loan, can be deducted if the second home is used primarily for personal as opposed to business use and is leased out to third parties for fewer than fifteen days a year.

If, however, the second home is leased out for fifteen days or more, but the homeowner also uses it for fourteen or more days per year, or more than ten percent of the total days leased to others (whichever is greater), the amount allowed to be deducted by the homeowner is limited to the equivalent of the total amount of rental income for the year.

If the second home of the homeowner is used fewer than fourteen days per year, or less than ten percent of the time that the home is leased out during the year, all allowable deductions treating the second home as a business expense are available.

These rules are constantly subject to change. Obviously, specific advice from a qualified tax advisor is recommended prior to determining which of the categories discussed above will apply to the tax effect of the second home.

THE HOME OFFICE

More than ever before, certain homeowners are operating a business or professional practice out of their homes. Aside from a means of consolidating overhead, this also provides the homeowner with a completely separate category of deductible expenses not otherwise allowed for in the use of a home.

Home Office Test

Prior to any tax advantages being allowed, a homeowner, to qualify, must satisfy the IRS that the home office is used exclusively and regularly for activities related to business and be either (1) the principal place of business; or (2) a place to meet clients, customers, or patients; or (3) located in a free-standing structure. An additional requirement exists when the homeowner is not self-employed but works as an employee. In this case, the home office must be a condition of employment and be for the convenience of the employer rather than the employee.

Do not assume that the definition of a home office as previously given can be as simple as it sounds. The IRS has specific rulings and case law that definitively deal with each one of these requirements. If a homeowner is considering placing his business within his home, the matter should be thoroughly discussed with a tax advisor so that all the criteria can be definitively met.

Allowable Deductions There are certain operating expenses for a home office that are wholly deductible if they constitute *direct home business expenses*. These are defined as any type of home office expense that would otherwise be a standard homeowner's expense, if not for the office being contained within the home.

Other types of deductible expenses for the home office are the type of *straight business expenses* that are typically deductible by any type of business. These may include business equipment purchases or rentals, professional dues, entertainment and public relations costs, salaries to employees and attendant payroll taxes, and so forth.

The difference between straight business expenses and direct home business expenses is that straight business expenses are not subject to any type of home office deduction limitation. The IRS, however, places a limit on the amount of direct home office expenses that the homeowner would otherwise be able to deduct. That is, the deductible amount of direct home office expenses cannot total more than the gross income of the business.

A third category of deductibility regarding the home office is *indirect home business expenses*. These are considered utilities, real estate taxes, home/loan interest payments, and any casualty loss. The portion of these expenses that can be taken as a business deduction depends upon how much of the home is for business and how much is for purely residential use. That is, if 35 percent of the home is used for business concerns, then 35 percent of the aforementioned types of home costs is deductible as an indirect home office expense.

Non-Allowable Deductions Generally, any type of expense that is related to the personal use section of the home is not deductible as a home office expense. Anytime an area of the home is used for personal reasons, it is considered an area that is non-exclusive to the business, and the expense cannot be deducted.

Depreciation Another type of home office deduction is depreciation. Although subject to rather specific rules and formulas, the homeowner is able to depreciate any portion of the property associated with the home office.

The homeowner is also able to depreciate any personal property kept in the home that is used solely in connection with the work being done in the home office. This is usually taken as a straight business expense. As in normal business situations, the depreciation factor in the home office is merely considered a tax device that spreads out the cost of the business asset or capital expenditure over the useful life of the particular item involved.

Sale of the Home Office When a home that has been used both as a home and as an office is sold, in essence two sales are occurring—one for the residence and one for the home office. The tax rules pertaining to the sale of both of these separate yet connected items can be somewhat complex, depending upon the terms and method of the sale and whether a new home or home office is subsequently purchased. Competent and specific tax advice is strongly recommended if the homeowner is anticipating selling his home office.

Other Home Office Considerations   The homeowner should make sure that any restrictive covenants, zoning restrictions, and applicable licensing requirements are met before trying to establish a home office. Even though the IRS home office test may be met, if the lack of local authority to conduct a business out of the home is not procured, it could severely undermine the taxpayer's position that the home office is a legitimate business and operating in accord with all legal requirements. Usually, a telephone call or visit to the local city planning office will provide the homeowner enough information to determine whether his particular type of home business will be permitted.

Finally, the IRS is notorious for closely scrutinizing home office deductions and depreciations. Accordingly, the homeowner who is claiming various deductions and depreciations pursuant to the existence of a home office must be prepared, better than most taxpayers, to prove his case.

8

Insurance

Home insurance consists of two basic categories: casualty and liability. Both of these types of coverage are discussed in this chapter, as are other insurance-related considerations.

THE POLICY Broadly defined, an insurance policy is a legal contract in which the insurance company, for a price, assumes the liability or risk of the insured and promises to pay a certain sum of money or other type of benefit if the insured suffers a loss or incurs damage within the scope of the policy.

Since an insurance policy is a legally binding contract, the rights and obligations of the parties to the policy are governed by basic principles of contract law. Simply put, both parties to the contract, the insurer and the insured, must give their acquiescence to the policy, and, further, the policy must be based upon binding legal consideration. The policy's general consideration is the money paid for the coverage provided.

Since the insurance business is regulated by law to a certain degree, certain provisions in the policy may be required or prohibited. However, in the absence of any type of law to the contrary, an insurance policy is valid and binding if its terms are enforceable under general contract law. For instance, if the language of the insurance policy is clear and concise, neither party can attempt to modify the terms or change the construction of the terminology of the policy. That is, the legal principle governing the construction of insurance contracts is that the intention of the parties controls, as is the rule in general contract law.

If there happens to be an addendum or a subsequent revision to the original policy, and there is a conflict between the original policy and this addendum, in most cases it is the provisions of the addendum that will control.

Another general rule of contract law that applies to insurance policies can be stated as follows: If the terminology contained within the policy is confusing or uncertain, and the parties' intent is not readily ascertainable by a reading of the policy, any interpretation of the policy's coverage will be construed against the insurance company. This is due to the fact that it was the insurer's policy that caused the ambiguity to exist.

As a corollary to this rule, any type of exclusion or exemption from an insurance policy, or limitations on the general amount of coverage involved, will also be construed strictly against the insurance company.

An insurance policy may be modified if agreed upon by the insurer and the insured. Unless a law exists that absolutely requires the change to be in writing, any amendment or modification of the policy can either be in writing or verbal. Obviously, it is better to have any type of change in the original policy be in writing, in the event that a dispute later arises with regard to the terms of the modification.

An insurance policy may be reformed or changed if it can be shown that the insurer and the insured made a mutual mistake with regard to the coverage that the insurer provides. For instance, if a homeowner enters into a casualty insurance policy and lists the incorrect street address of the home being covered, and the insurance company does not notice the mistake and enters into a policy to this effect, any subsequent damage to the home will in all likelihood be covered by the insurance policy despite the mistake in the address in the policy. A reformation of the policy will usually be allowed if a mistake of both of the parties has occurred, and the intent of both the insured and the insurer was not reflected in the written policy.

Also, an insurance policy may be renewed if the insured continues to make payments even after the policy has been formally terminated, assuming that the insurer accepts the payments and takes no further action to terminate the policy. Usually, the procedures regarding the right to renew an existing insurance policy are specifically set forth in the policy itself.

Cancellation of an insurance policy can be made by either the insured or the insurer if the other party to the policy has committed fraud or misrepresentation. If the insurer has declared bankruptcy, the insurer may similarly cancel the policy. Bankruptcy is enough of a material change to terminate the contract, based upon changes in the original conditions.

Most types of policies for homeowner's insurance specifically contain a litany of the different types of circumstances that will allow the insurer to terminate the policy without the acquiescence of the insured. However, certain state laws may expressly limit the effect of these cancellation provisions and give the homeowner various legal rights to avoid any attempted cancellation of the policy. This is based on the fact that the law does not usually favor the unilateral forfeiture of an insurance policy that is otherwise entered into on a valid and legal basis.

If the homeowner sells his home, the general rule is that any type of insurance policy currently in place is not transferable to the new owner. That is, the policy is not transferable to a new insured without the consent of the insurer and complete compliance by the new owner with the terms of the existing policy with respect to any assignment rules the policy may have.

CASUALTY INSURANCE

A homeowner's casualty insurance policy protects the homeowner from certain types of losses to the home itself. These types of losses stem from natural and otherwise unavoidable elements such as fire, storm damage, theft, and the like. The type and scope of coverage that is available to a homeowner encompasses a broad spectrum of availability, which will be discussed shortly.

Required by Lender

As discussed in the previous chapters, a lender who has obtained a security interest in the home in exchange for lending the homeowner the money to purchase the home does have an economic interest to prevent any damage or destruction to the home. In this regard, both the homeowner and the lender have an insurable interest in the home, and either is entitled to enter into an insurance policy protecting themselves from casualty losses.

Almost all mortgages or deeds of trust contain a specific provision that requires the homeowner to maintain adequate casualty insurance on the home at all times. The amount of the coverage is also set by the lender, usually up to the amount of the loan amount. For instance, if the home is worth $100,000 (not including the lot), and the amount of the loan is $65,000, the lender will require at least $65,000 of casualty coverage to protect its security.

As the loan balance is reduced, the insurable interest of the lender also is reduced. Once the loan on the home has been paid, there is no legal requirement for the homeowner to have casualty insurance. However, the homeowner would be totally at risk without such casualty coverage.

Type and Amount of Coverage

There are several different types of standard casualty insurance policies available. One of the least expensive and basic forms of casualty insurance is the *standard form* of coverage on the dwelling and the personal property kept inside. The homeowner determines the value of his personal property, such as furniture, appliances, and clothes, and the value of the home minus the value of the lot. The insurer under this type of coverage will reimburse the homeowner (minus any deductible) for the value of these items for standard types of potential causes. These typically include: fire, lightning, storms, wind, explosions, riots, aircraft accidents, smoke damage, theft, vandalism, volcanic eruption, or motor vehicle accidents affecting the home.

Another type of casualty insurance that is popular, but costs somewhat more, is the *broad form* of coverage. Along with the items covered in the standard form casualty policy, broad form of coverage also provides protection from falling objects (meteorites); snow, ice, or sleet damage; water or steam damage from discharging plumbing, air conditioning, or household appliances; damage from the hot water or air conditioning system; damage from freezing of a plumbing, heating, or air conditioning unit; and damage resulting from any type of electrical surge.

The next step up of casualty insurance coverage is called the *special form* policy. This type of coverage insures the homeowner for all types of perils except flood, earthquake, war, nuclear accident, and any specific exemptions otherwise contained in the policy. This type of complete casualty coverage costs more than the previous two types of policies.

There is also a type of homeowner's casualty insurance that pertains to condominium owners. It provides for the replacement value of any lost personal property and liability insurance coverage (discussed below). Since the condominium is usually one unit in a building containing many units, this type of coverage with regard to potential casualty losses usually suffices. Any type of permanent installation of personal property within the condominium by the owner usually requires some type of addendum to the policy to make sure that this particular item is covered.

Another type of homeowner's casualty insurance pertains solely to older homes. This type of coverage only provides a certain specific cash value in the event of a loss, as opposed to the replacement cost of the home, should it be destroyed.

This type of coverage exists because most insurance companies are not willing to enter into a policy that provides replacement cost, due to the fact that many older homes would be difficult and overly expensive to duplicate. The replacement cost could be two or three times the market value of the home. Hence, the insurance company is only willing to assign a specific cash value to the home and reimburse the homeowner for any type of insured loss up to the amount of the home's cash value as stated in the policy.

Coverage Limitations As previously indicated, most homeowner casualty insurance policies contain a specific limitation on coverage. This limitation is usually the replacement value of the home, or a specifically agreed upon dollar amount that, in the event of a total loss, the insurance company is obligated to pay the homeowner. Even some policies that require the insurer to provide the homeowner with total replacement cost contain a specific limit on the amount that the insurer is required to pay.

If the homeowner believes that the replacement cost or value of his home has increased since the original policy was entered into, the homeowner should modify his existing coverage and enter into a new policy so as to provide adequate coverage for the increased value of the home. This is not a legal requirement, but merely a practical concern that the homeowner should keep in mind with regard to his casualty insurance coverage.

Inflation Index Certain types of homeowner insurance policies contain an inflation index clause. This means that the stated value of the home in the insurance policy is adjusted to reflect or match a specific inflation index, such as the federal government's consumer price index. This provision gives the policy an element of flexibility and protects the homeowner in the event that the value of the home increases substantially during the time of the policy and negates the need for periodically increasing the amount of coverage.

Other Types of Coverage
Flood damage to a home is almost always excluded from casualty homeowner insurance. If the home is located in a flood plain or flood zone, and the homeowner wishes to insure against water damage stemming from a potential flood, it may be very difficult or impossible to obtain that type of coverage.

However, there is a national flood insurance program from certain private insurance companies that may be available to the homeowner. Generally, the homeowner must live within a certain flood-prone area that complies with governmental guidelines for insurable flood prevention coverage. The premiums depend greatly on the degree of risk of flooding in any particular area and the location of the particular home.

Another cause of potential damage to a home that is rarely covered is earthquake. If the homeowner desires earthquake coverage, it must be specifically entered into on a separate policy by a company that offers it, which in itself is somewhat of a rarity.

Certain states have what are termed *fair access to insurance requirements*, also known as *fair plan insurance*. These are, in essence, insurance coverage for homeowners in what are considered high risk areas. They are operated by private companies that share the potential loss and profits in proportion to the share of the total business in their respective states. Fair plan insurance costs more than other types of casualty insurance, but may be the only way in which the homeowner is able to obtain casualty insurance due to the location of the home in a particularly high risk area.

Homeowners who live in an area prone to high crime may have a difficult time obtaining casualty insurance to cover burglary and vandalism. There does exist a federal crime insurance program, which, if the homeowner qualifies, provides an insurance policy for losses due to burglary or vandalism. Most insurance agents can direct the homeowner to the proper government authority to discuss the possibility of obtaining this type of casualty insurance.

Personal Property Floater
Aside from a policy provision that protects the contents of the home, a homeowner can also obtain what is known as a *personal property floater*. This insures certain specific and expensive items, such as fur coats, silverware, antiques, or artwork. This type of separate policy or addendum to a standard policy contains a detailed description of the personal property that is insured and guarantees total replacement cost.

An alternative to obtaining a personal property floater is for the homeowner to buy additional *blanket personal property coverage* for a specific category of protection, such as extended amounts of coverage for any jewelry located in the home. However, this type of increase in personal property coverage usually contains a monetary limit as to the amount recoverable for the particular item damaged or destroyed. It is up to the homeowner to determine which is the more desirable coverage, depending upon his personal level of risk and the type and value of personal property involved.

Deductibles All insurance policies contain what is termed a *deductible*. This is the amount stated in the policy for which the homeowner assumes the risk. For instance, if $4,500 of hail damage has occurred to the home, and the homeowner has a $500 deductible, the insurance company is responsible for reimbursing the homeowner for only $4,000. As you might guess, the higher the deductible, the lower the premium.

LIABILITY INSURANCE

Liability insurance, also known as premises liability insurance, is insurance that protects the homeowner for any type of claim by anyone injured or damaged on the homeowner's property. Liability insurance is procured to prevent the homeowner from suffering a loss, usually by way of a lawsuit, by a third party who is hurt or damaged due to the negligence of the homeowner or his family.

Even if a third party files a lawsuit against the homeowner for damages, and the homeowner is successful in defending the lawsuit, the attorney fees and costs involved (without the existence of liability insurance) could cause severe economic hardship on the homeowner. A liability insurance company would be obligated to defend the homeowner for any type of claim made by a third party against the homeowner for injuries sustained on the property or as a result of the homeowner's occupation of the property.

What is Covered Most premises liability insurance on a home protects a homeowner from claims based on the homeowner's *negligence* as to third parties. Negligence is legally defined as a duty that one has to another, which is breached, to the damage or detriment of another.

Liability insurance protects any members of the homeowner's family who live in the home. The coverage is not necessarily limited to accidents that occur on the home's premises, but also if the homeowner or his family causes injury to another or another's property. This typically includes any pets or animals owned by the homeowner.

As an example, if someone is walking along the sidewalk in front of your home, and the wind knocks a tree branch down from your tree and strikes the individual, causing him injury, the homeowner can be held responsible. Even though the homeowner did not know that the limb was going to break, the mere fact that the homeowner was the owner of the tree creates an obligation of the homeowner with regard to any injured bystander.

Other examples involving cases where the homeowner's liability insurance come into play include: someone slipping and falling on ice accumulated on the driveway; a neighbor's child being harmed when he falls from a swingset located in the homeowner's yard; a swimming accident in the homeowner's pool; or the homeowner's dog biting a neighbor.

If the homeowner is adjudged to be liable, he will be responsible for all medical bills incurred by the injured party. Further, if an individual suffers a loss and is unable to resume work as a result of an injury occurring on the homeowner's property, the homeowner can be held liable for any lost wages or earnings of that individual, if it can be shown that the wages were lost as a direct result of the injuries sustained. Obviously, if the injury incapacitates someone for a long period of time, the amount of potential damages can escalate rapidly.

Aside from these specific types of losses, the injured party may also be entitled to compensation for pain and suffering. Although this amount is not ascertainable to a specific degree, juries have been known to award large sums of money if the pain is severe or permanent in nature.

Non-Covered Items Recognize that any homeowner will not be covered by his liability insurance policy for damages or injuries resulting from intentional acts of the homeowner. Liability insurance does not give the homeowner a license to injure; it protects the homeowner for the type of injuries sustained by the homeowner's negligence, or where the injury was unpreventable, as in a strict liability case.

If the homeowner is operating a business out of his home, acts or negligent acts of any employees of the homeowner are not covered under the typical homeowner's liability insurance policy. Further, a homeowner's liability insurance policy will in all likelihood not cover vacation homes or investment property in the name of the homeowner, unless separate coverage for those properties is specifically obtained. Malpractice or products liability insurance is not included in most home business insurance policies. These coverages must be obtained separately.

Umbrella Policies An *umbrella liability insurance policy* generally extends or increases the amount of liability coverage to $100 million or more. This type of umbrella policy also covers any type of damage or liability stemming from automobiles in the homeowner's name. The term *umbrella* stands for the comprehensive aspect of the coverage.

This type of umbrella policy provides coverage that is much broader than a typical homeowner policy, and also covers bodily injury and property damage, false arrest, wrongful eviction, liability, slander, defamation of character, or invasion of privacy claims brought against the homeowner. These policies are designed for the homeowner who desires the maximum coverage available.

HOME OFFICE INSURANCE

Most standard homeowner's liability insurance policies do not cover any type of injuries or damages that are work-related. If the homeowner is conducting a business out of his home, additional protection should be obtained. There are two avenues to take when insuring the homeowner's home business.

Business Rider Policy The homeowner may desire to purchase a *business rider* to his existing homeowner's policy. In addition to the existing homeowner's insurance policy, a business rider covers the type of losses typically and potentially involved in a business. As a general proposition, if one-fifth or less of the homeowner's residence is devoted to his home business, this type of rider policy is available.

It must also be demonstrated to the insurance company that there is no type of inherently risky business activity occurring in the home, such as the use of dangerous equipment or machinery, chemicals, or numerous employees.

Home business rider policies are designed to cover the smaller type of home office situation. The policy will likely contain a description of the business activity that is covered and a brief description of the business furnishings and equipment that are insured.

Special Home Office Coverage If the homeowner's business does not qualify for the type of rider policy mentioned in the previous section, the business may be insured by a completely separate policy. The type and amount of coverage involved depends primarily on what type of business is being conducted out of the home. The greater the potential risk (as decided by the insurer), the greater the cost of the policy. The policy would only cover specific liabilities that result from the operation of the business itself.

Other Types of Home Office Coverage The homeowner who is conducting a business out of his home should not depend upon his business coverage policy or home business rider policy to compensate employees for injuries suffered on the job. It is the employer's responsibility and liability to pay for any medical costs, loss of income, or other damages in the event of an injured employee, unless worker's compensation coverage is in effect at the time of the injury. Most states require worker's compensation insurance to be in place for all employees.

Home business policies do not cover damages of computer equipment if the damages stem from some type of malfunctioning electrical circuitry or electrical surge. Damage to any computer software will similarly not be covered for these types of incidents, although the typical types of covered peril, such as theft and fire, usually provide for compensation.

If the home office has an extensive business inventory, insurance must also be procured in the event that some type of accident occurs that damages the inventory. That is, inventory is considered a separate item from other types of insured personal property of the business.

Another type of insurance that the homeowner should consider when conducting a business out of his home is *interruption of business* coverage. If there is substantial damage to the premises, any resulting loss of business income will not be covered, unless this type of insurance is in place.

MORTGAGE INSURANCE

Private Mortgage Insurance

If a conventional home mortgage is obtained by a buyer, but he is not able to provide a substantial down payment (typically twenty percent or more of the purchase price), the buyer will most likely be required to have private mortgage insurance on the loan.

The lender agrees to make the loan for a small down payment, but a private insurance company insures part of the loan. Usually, the homeowner pays for the insurance in one of two ways: the homeowner may pay a premium equal to a certain percentage of the declining balance of the loan, typically one-half of one percent of the loan balance. Or the homeowner will be required to pay a set premium for a particular term, which is usually a small percentage of the loan. The homeowner will also have to pay a one-time fee to the lender to handle the paperwork in putting the insurance in place.

If the buyer should default on the loan, the lender submits a claim to the insurance company for the unpaid principal and interest payments, including any reasonable legal fees or repairs to the home stemming from the buyer's default.

FHA-Insured Mortgages

As discussed in the chapter on financing, another type of insurance that is used with purchasing a home is Federal Housing Administration (FHA) insured loans.

This type of insurance stems from the FHA promising the lender that if the buyer does not make the payments, the FHA will purchase the mortgage from the lender. This obviously reduces the risk for the lender and, accordingly, the terms of the loan are made more attractive to the buyer.

The Federal Housing Administration puts a limit on how much interest lenders can charge on FHA-insured loans, with the maximum rate often being below the general market rate on conventional loans. The homeowner is required to pay an insurance premium fee on the FHA mortgage loan, usually an amount equal to one-half of one percent of the loan balance annually.

Mortgage Life Insurance

Mortgage life insurance can be defined as a type of life insurance in which the homeowner pays a specific amount, usually monthly, for coverage that will pay any remaining balance of a first mortgage loan on the home if the insured homeowner should die. The amount of the premium often remains the same during the life of the loan.

Of course, the mortgage loan balance is being steadily reduced as time goes by, and having mortgage life insurance during the last five to ten years of the loan may not be cost beneficial. However, it is one method for the homeowner to insure that if he should die and his ability to pay the mortgage loan be gone, the home will be owned free and clear by his heirs. Mortgage life insurance is especially attractive to young couples during the early years of the mortgage.

9

The Home's Legal Environment

There are several other legal definitions and topics that affect home ownership. Some have been referred to in previous chapters, while others are presented here for the first time. A working knowledge of these areas will prove beneficial to the homeowner if any potential situation happens to arise involving these subjects.

USE RESTRICTIONS ON THE HOME

Although the premise of home ownership in the United States is that the property may be used as the owner sees fit, various restrictions, both privately and governmentally enforced, do exist, which will limit how the home can be used. This section reviews such restrictions and limitations.

Zoning

Zoning on residential property can be defined as the power given to a municipality or local government body to dictate the extent of home use within the boundaries of the municipality, including any surrounding buffer zones. Generally, the different types of zoning include residential, commercial, industrial, and agricultural.

Any type of residential use of real estate must be, with some exceptions, within a residential zoning area. If an individual is considering constructing a home within a zoned area, he must determine whether the type of home to be constructed complies with local zoning restrictions and classifications.

An exception to zoning compliance laws is the *theory of non-conforming use*. In essence, this means that if the owner of a piece of property is using the property in a certain manner that, due to subsequently adopted zoning restrictions, is no longer in conformity with current zoning laws, the owner cannot be legally ordered to discontinue that type of use or activity without being paid in full for the value of the property. Otherwise, the changing of the type of use permitted for the property pursuant to subsequently enacted zoning laws would constitute an unconstitutional taking of property.

If a particular residential property is located in a zone that prohibits homes, the homeowner may apply for a *variance*. In essence, the homeowner applies for permission from the applicable local government body to deviate from the existing zoning code. It is incumbent upon the homeowner to show that the variance requested will not have a detrimental effect on nearby property values or reduce the existing use of surrounding areas. A variance is most often used for a minor or modest deviation from the requirements of the zoning code.

If a homeowner is applying for a more radical inconsistent use of the property within a zoning area, the homeowner can apply for a *zone change*. Again, the homeowner must show that the requested change has no detrimental effect on the surrounding areas, with regard to either use or affected value. Adjacent property owners will usually have an opportunity to express their opinions on the desirability of the requested change.

Restrictive Covenants A *restrictive covenant* is a non-governmental or private agreement that restricts the use of the home. It is usually set forth in a controlling master deed and *runs with the land*. This means that all subsequent owners of the home are bound by the restrictive covenants.

In most situations, restrictive covenants are used in new or newer residential subdivisions. They often require that a specific type of home be constructed, including minimum square footage, architectural design, and the like. Restrictive covenants may also limit certain types of involvements or activities on the homeowner's property. For example: outdoor repair work on automobiles, above ground pools greater than a certain size, fences in the front yard, and outside radio antennas or satellite dishes are all likely to be prohibited.

The purpose of restrictive covenants is to make sure that all the homeowners in the particular area affected reap the benefits of maintaining quality control over the homes of the other property owners. Whenever a homeowner is considering purchasing a new or fairly new home, the question should always be raised as to what type of restrictive covenants exist so as to not mislead the homeowner as to exactly what is prohibited and what is not prohibited within the neighborhood. Most competent real estate brokers will provide a prospective buyer with a copy of the restrictive covenants currently in force.

Flood Plains Some cities and towns have designated, through zoning, an area known as the *flood plain district*. The building of new homes (or other real estate construction), is not legally permitted within this area.

The purpose of flood plain zoning restrictions is to protect people who might otherwise build or live near a flood plain, unaware of the potential dangers and liability involved. If a home is constructed and then subsequently declared to be within a flood plain, the municipality cannot prevent the homeowner from remaining there, as was mentioned previously with the theory of non-conforming use.

Home Businesses   Anytime a homeowner is considering conducting a full- or part-time business out of his home, he will, in all likelihood, be in violation of the applicable zoning laws. Most zoning ordinances for residential areas do not allow businesses to be conducted within such an area.

Accordingly, prior to anything else, the special use homeowner should obtain a zoning variance or other available permit excepting the activity from applicable zoning laws to allow the specific type of business to be conducted out of his home. The homeowner has the burden of showing that the business will have no detrimental effect on the surrounding area. All surrounding property owners will have an opportunity to voice their concerns as to whether they think the zoning variance or special use permit should be granted.

Construction Permits   Anytime a substantial or permanent improvement is to be made on an existing home, a construction permit must be applied for and obtained. Without such a permit, the local government entity can either have the improvement removed or levy a fine for failure to obtain a permit.

Construction permits are generally required so that the taxable value of the home can be adjusted accordingly. By maintaining a system of formal checks on improvements to existing homes, the local taxing authorities are potentially able to increase real estate tax revenues. Also, this system allows the government to make sure any such improvements are built in compliance with local building codes.

Easements   An *easement* is a non-possessory interest in real estate, which allows the non-owner to use the owner's property for a certain purpose. Easements as to residential real estate usually are created at the time the home is built by a specific granting of easement rights to utility or telephone companies. These easements allow such companies to place, maintain, and repair their equipment (usually underground cables) on the homeowner's property. The homeowner is obligated to see that these easements are continually allowed and not disrupted.

LIENS AND OTHER ENCUMBRANCES   Liens and other types of encumbrances on the ownership of a home must also be understood and appreciated. The homeowner should distinguish between liens and mortgages. The types of liens and encumbrances discussed in this section are non-voluntary in nature, while mortgages, trust deeds, and the like are voluntary in nature since they are given with the acquiescence of the homeowner. Liens, on the other hand, can be placed on the homeowner's property without the consent of the homeowner.

Judgment Liens   A *judgment lien* occurs when a judgment (court order) against the homeowner has been obtained. A judgment lien is an interest in the homeowner's property for the amount of the judgment.

Prior to a judgment lien being created, a lawsuit must be filed against the homeowner. If a decision is made by the court against the home-owner, a judgment lien is created. Generally, a party who has a judgment lien against a home is able to proceed with enforcing the judgment lien by conducting a sheriff's sale, with any buyer of the home taking title subject to all existing mortgages, liens, and other security interests against the property. Payment of the judgment lien or the filing of bankruptcy by the homeowner negates the judgment liens.

Child Support Liens In many jurisdictions, an ongoing obligation to pay child support by the homeowner constitutes a continuing lien on the property. That is, as security for the child support being paid on a timely basis, a lien will be created by law and remains in effect even though the homeowner is totally current with his child support payments.

If the homeowner desires to sell, transfer, or refinance his property, and remove or subordinate the child support lien so as to allow this to occur, it can generally be effected voluntarily between the homeowner and his ex-spouse. However, if the ex-spouse is not willing to enter into a subordination or release agreement in this regard, a court order to this effect can be obtained if the homeowner is current with his child support. Again, the child support lien merely gives the support recipient security for payment of the child support during the time in which it is owed, which can last for several years.

Construction Liens A *construction lien*, also known as a mechanic's lien, comes into play when the homeowner has had some type of permanent improvement or work done on his home and has not paid the individual or company for the labor or material provided. Construction liens were referred to in Chapter 6. (There is an example of a Construction Lien in the Appendix.)

Although local laws vary substantially, a construction lien can usually be created by affidavit, which is filed against the home in the applicable local recording office. To enforce a construction lien, the individual or company who created the lien must foreclose. The construction lien is usually subordinate to any other existing mortgages or deeds of trust, thus making it somewhat difficult for the construction lien holder to enforce his interest without considerable expense.

Recognize that the individual or company who is entitled to file a construction lien for non-payment may do so without the homeowner's consent. However, the lien must generally be filed within a certain period of time, usually a few months, subsequent to the work being completed. If that time has passed and no construction lien has been filed, the lien has no legal effect.

The homeowner involved in a home construction project should always make sure that all subcontractors and suppliers are paid. This can be done with checks made payable to both the general contractor and the subcontractor. The homeowner can also pay the subcontractors or suppliers directly.

The homeowner should never rely on the general contractor to see that all subcontractors and suppliers are paid. If the general contractor does not make payment, the homeowner will usually have to pay these subcontractors or suppliers himself, thus creating a potential case for double payment. Of course, the homeowner would be able to proceed with a lawsuit against the general contractor for not paying his subcontractors or suppliers, but sometimes the general contractor may be without assets, bankrupt, or simply gone.

Tax Liens   There are two basic types of involuntary tax liens that can be placed on the homeowner's property. The first kind is the delinquent payment of property tax. The non-payment of property taxes in most areas constitutes an automatic lien against the home and will remain as such until paid.

If the homeowner has not paid any owed income taxes, the Internal Revenue Service may place an income tax lien on the homeowner's property without first proceeding with a lawsuit and obtaining a judgment, as would be the case if a typical creditor were involved. If necessary, the Internal Revenue Service may proceed with enforcement of the tax lien by way of a foreclosure action or sheriff's sale.

Lis Pendens   A notice of *lis pendens* is a document filed in the applicable public registry to put individuals on notice that a certain parcel of real estate is currently involved in or subject to a lawsuit. Anytime legal action is commenced concerning the disposition of real estate, a notice of lis pendens will be filed by the party who initiates the lawsuit.

The purpose of a notice of lis pendens is to advise prospective buyers that the title to the property may be affected by a court ruling. If a title search reveals the existence of a lis pendens notice, a buyer should make further inquiry regarding the status of the lawsuit that caused the notice of lis pendens to be filed.

Effect on Transfer   Any of the previously mentioned liens and encumbrances on the home effectively prohibit the transfer of the home. No buyer will be willing to accept title while liens are against the home, as they could potentially be enforced against the new homeowner.

It is the homeowner who must remove these types of lien encumbrances so as to allow the effective transfer of the home. In general, judgment liens must be *satisfied*, which entails filing a *satisfaction of judgment* by the judgment creditor, indicating that the amount owed pursuant to the judgment has been paid in full.

As mentioned, child support liens can be negated by court order or by voluntary acquiescence of the child support recipient. Local laws govern the exact procedure that must be taken, and must be considered prior to attempting to release a child support lien at the time of sale.

With regard to construction liens, the lien holder must file a *release of lien* in the office in which the original lien was placed, indicating that the lien has been paid in full.

Similarly, the payment of any past due property taxes automatically cancels any lien on the title to the home. Income tax debts that have risen to the status of a lien on the home are removed in a like manner. The homeowner should always obtain written documentation that the liens being released are, in fact, no longer in effect.

BOUNDARY DISPUTES AND ADJOINING HOMEOWNERS

Sometimes a homeowner becomes involved in a boundary dispute with a neighbor. This section deals with the applicable factors and legal terminology if the homeowner happens to become embroiled in such a dispute.

Survey

As mentioned in the previous chapters, when an individual purchases a home, title insurance or an attorney's opinion on the condition of the title is involved. Recognize, however, that this does not necessarily mean the title insurance company is insuring that the boundaries to the home are what they appear to be. In fact, most title insurance companies specifically list this as an exception in the policy.

For the homeowner to assure himself of the exact boundaries of the home or land to be purchased, he must obtain a survey by a qualified survey company that specifically locates and guarantees the boundaries of the home. Although a survey can cost several hundred dollars above and beyond the title insurance premium, it may be worth it if the homeowner is particularly concerned about the specific parameters of the property being purchased and wishes to obtain some type of professional assurance as to its boundary lines. In addition, the lender may require a survey before approving the loan request.

Nuisance

It is a basic principle of real estate law that every homeowner may enjoy reasonable and lawful use of his property subject to the corresponding right of adjoining property owners to enjoy their property. As long as one homeowner is not creating a *nuisance*, he may do anything he desires as to utilization of the home (subject to applicable zoning laws and restrictive covenants).

The test with regard to the permissible use of a home is whether the usage by the homeowner is a reasonable exercise of property ownership so as to not deprive the adjacent homeowner of his usage rights.

For example, if one homeowner has several dogs in his backyard, which are constantly barking and harassing the neighbors, and no particular city ordinance is being violated, an adjacent homeowner may nevertheless have a cause of action in court for a nuisance. If he can demonstrate that his neighbor's dogs are keeping him and his family from enjoying their backyard, the court may enter an injunction against the homeowner to prohibit or limit the presence of the dogs.

Another example of a nuisance is if one homeowner has a large burning incinerator in his yard, and the prevailing winds cause smoke and soot to flow constantly into his neighbor's yard, thus limiting his ability to enjoy his home.

A nuisance type of lawsuit is very much dependent on the particular facts and the amount of damage sustained. In general, the courts will try to *balance the equities* of the respective homeowners' use of their property. This involves determining whether the use being complained of is unreasonable, or the consequences of the use are truly detrimental to the adjoining homeowner.

Trespassing Trespassing can be either a civil act or a criminal offense. Criminal trespassing makes it illegal for an individual to enter another's property. Civil trespass is a cause of action in which one party is requesting a judgment amount for specific damages due to another's unauthorized use or occupancy of the homeowner's property.

In general, all that is necessary to bring a cause of action for trespass is to show that another person is occupying, using, or traversing another's property without the owner's express or implied permission. Of course, the amount of damages sustained may be negligible, but nevertheless the civil cause of action for trespass does exist and is available to the homeowner.

Encroachments An *encroachment* between adjoining property owners is where the property of one adjoining land owner is not necessarily located on the property of the adjoining homeowner; rather, the homeowner's property is being affected by the type of encroachment involved.

For instance, if a tree is growing on the homeowner's property and the branches are overhanging into a neighbor's yard, the neighboring homeowner will, with some exceptions, have the legal right to remove the overhanging branches that cross over onto his property. In effect, an encroachment is a trespass of property owned by the adjoining homeowner.

If, however, a tree is growing squarely on the property dividing line, it would generally be held to be common property of both owners and neither may destroy or injure the tree without the consent of the other. However, if one of the homeowners believes that the common property tree is damaging his property, such as preventing any growth of grass, or harming his roof, that homeowner does have the right to protect his property by taking any necessary steps to correct the situation.

It should be recognized that a homeowner who is injured or damaged by an encroachment by an adjoining homeowner may remedy the situation himself without resorting to specific legal action, if in fact the encroachment amounts to a private nuisance only affecting his particular property.

Another type of encroachment occurs when a homeowner changes the grade or lay of the land on his property, resulting in water drainage occurring in a different fashion so as to affect detrimentally the adjacent homeowner. The damaged homeowner may have legal recourse if he can show that the actions of his neighbor caused the change in drainage that resulted in property damage to his home.

OTHER METHODS OF INVOLUNTARY TAKING

Even if the homeowner has no mortgages, deeds of trust, judgment liens, child support liens, or tax liens against the property, there are other situations in which the property can be taken from the homeowner, both with and without compensation.

Adverse Possession

Adverse possession is a specific right in most jurisdictions that allows a non-owner to acquire title to real estate by means of unauthorized occupancy of the property for a certain period of time. Generally, the non-owner must occupy the property as if he owns it; that is, openly, continuously, and without the express written or implied consent of the owner.

The adverse possessor must occupy the property continuously but not necessarily constantly (twenty-four hours a day) for a specific length of time. Usually that period is anywhere between ten and twenty years, depending upon local law.

If the non-owner does occupy the property as his own for the necessary period of time, he can make a claim to the courts as an adverse possessor and require the courts to enter an order declaring him to be the lawful owner. No compensation is awarded to the previous owner.

Adverse possession appears to be a legal way of acquiring land illegally. However, the purpose of adverse possession is to discourage non-occupying owners from not monitoring or using their property. The theory of adverse possession is to encourage full and efficient use of the land by the owner and to discourage any dilatory enforcement of the property owner's rights. It also is a specific means of deciding title disputes between owners and non-authorized occupiers.

An owner should make periodic inspection of his property to check against any potential adverse possessors. It should be noted that, in most states, the mere posting of "No Trespassing" signs is not legally sufficient to protect the owner from an adverse possession claim.

Eminent Domain

Eminent domain is the power of the government, either state, federal, or local, to take private property for public use. The property owner is entitled to compensation for the property taken. If the government can demonstrate that the property must be taken to enhance the public good or to benefit public use, an owner has no choice but to transfer the property to the government.

For instance, if the homeowner's property is located along a street that the city desires to widen for the benefit of public transportation, the government will follow the necessary procedure, called the *condemnation proceeding,* to take the property. Even if only part of the property is taken, the government is legally required to reimburse the homeowner for the lost value of the property that remains.

Since the government must reimburse the property owner, any dispute with regard to eminent domain proceedings usually involves the actual amount of compensation. The homeowner may bring in real estate appraisal experts to prove that the value of the property taken is a certain amount, while the government will counter with its appraisers, stating that the value of the property is a lesser amount. In fact, trials often occur solely on this particular issue.

The important thing to remember, however, is that the homeowner has no legal right to retain the property being taken under the government's power of eminent domain. The only real issue is how much the homeowner will be paid as compensation.

THE HOME AND DIVORCE

If a couple obtains a divorce and one or both of them has an interest in the home, the home is subject to the property settlement of the divorce decree and can be divided up or transferred in many ways.

The particular method of ownership of the home will not be binding on the courts. That is, if the property is solely owned by one spouse, the other spouse still, in all likelihood, has a legal interest in the home depending upon the length of the marriage, contributions of the spouse, and other factors of the marriage. The court is not bound by how the title happens to be held but looks beyond that to determine what the particular parties' interests and contributions have been during the term of the marriage.

The property settlement may provide that, if both spouses are named on the title, one spouse is to *quitclaim* his interest to the other spouse so that the title results in being in the name of only one of the spouses. The divorce decree may provide that if the house is subsequently sold by the spouse who retains sole ownership, any equity realized from the sale may be divided between the ex-spouses. Again, this is dependent upon many things, including the duration of the marriage, contributions during the term of the marriage, custody considerations, and so on.

The court also has the option of ordering that the house be sold as soon as reasonably possible, with any equity to be distributed between the divorced spouses. This often occurs when neither spouse can continue to maintain the existing mortgage payments or does not desire to remain in the home.

In states that have community property laws, any property, including the home, acquired by either spouse and placed in either spouse's name during the term of the marriage, is considered community property and owned equally between the spouses. Community property does not include property acquired during the term of the marriage that is received by gift or inheritance to one of the spouses.

If the home is owned by either spouse prior to the marriage, it remains as his separate property during the term of the marriage and does not constitute community property, and, with some exceptions, the ownership of the home is not affected pursuant to the divorce decree and property settlement.

Please recall the $125,000 one-time tax exclusion rule regarding the sale of the home, as discussed in Chapter 7. If a couple is contemplating selling their home in connection with a divorce, it is probably best if the sale occurs after the divorce is final. That way, only one spouse will be bound by this one-time exclusion rule, and the other spouse can take advantage of this tax rule in the future.

THE HOME AND ESTATE CONSIDERATIONS

Several different things can occur with the disposition of a home upon the owner's death. As discussed in Chapter 5, if the property is held between the homeowner and another as joint tenants with rights of survivorship, the surviving owner (or owners) is automatically deemed to own the property, without being subject to any interest of the deceased or his heirs. The advantage of joint tenancy with rights of survivorship is that it generally does not have to be processed through probate to transfer title to any surviving joint tenants. Joint tenancy with rights of survivorship is the most common method for spouses to hold title to their home.

If the homeowner owns the home as a tenant in common, his interest is passed on to his heirs, either through the terms of his will or through the laws of succession in his state of domicile. His heirs will take the deceased tenant in common's interest, and then become tenants in common with any surviving tenant in common. Often, the surviving tenant in common will buy out the interest of the heirs of the deceased tenant in common, or some other type of agreement will be created during the probate procedure.

Another method of terminating an interest in a home at the time of death is the life estate, as discussed in Chapter 5. In a life estate, the homeowner transfers his property during his lifetime to another, but reserves a life estate in the home. The consequence is that the homeowner has the legal right to occupy and own the home, and all its attendant responsibilities and advantages, during his life. However, upon his death, the life estate is terminated and the transferor of the life estate then becomes the owner of the home. Life estates are often used between relatives who wish to avoid local inheritance tax or probate costs.

There are other methods of holding title to the home so as to avoid or minimize estate taxes and inheritance taxes. For instance, the property owned can be held by a trust with the trust's beneficiary allowed to occupy the home. A real estate attorney or trust officer should be consulted regarding the most advantageous type of trust ownership available as part of an overall estate plan.

BANKRUPTCY

A homeowner can sometimes be faced with a potential bankruptcy, or is involved in a bankruptcy proceeding by purchasing a home from a bankrupt seller.

Types of Bankruptcy

There are generally two types of bankruptcies that affect individuals. A Chapter 7 bankruptcy, also known as a straight bankruptcy, potentially discharges all debts except those from child support, alimony, taxes, and student loans less than five years old. In effect, it wipes the slate clean of most debts.

The other type of bankruptcy that a homeowner may be involved with is termed the Chapter 13 bankruptcy. Chapter 13 bankruptcy is a procedure whereby the debtor is employed or has dependable income. The debtor enters into a court-approved plan that repays the secured and unsecured creditors a certain percentage of the respective money owed.

Bankruptcy and the Homeowner Even in a Chapter 7 proceeding, a mortgage company is often able to obtain permission from the bankruptcy court to proceed either with a foreclosure action or to enter into an agreement where the debtor agrees to continue making his mortgage payment. For various reasons, since the lender is a secured creditor, it is in a stronger legal position to receive this type of authority from the court. Typically, the mortgage loan is either reaffirmed by the debtor or the debtor transfers a deed in lieu of foreclosure to the lender.

In a Chapter 7 bankruptcy, since many of the debtor's unsecured debts no longer need to be paid, the homeowner usually is able to enter into a *reaffirmation agreement* with the lender to make up any missed payments and recommence with paying the balance of the mortgage loan. This way, the bankrupt homeowner can retain ownership of the property.

In a Chapter 13 proceeding, the secured creditors, including the lender who has a security interest in the home, are usually paid 100 percent of their monies, while unsecured creditors receive much less.

As can be seen, bankruptcy can be an advantageous route to take by the homeowner, if in fact the homeowner has any equity to protect in his home and is otherwise unable to make the scheduled mortgage loan payments due to a large amount of unsecured debt, such as credit cards or other installment loan obligations.

Dealing with the Bankrupt Seller Often, after a bankruptcy is filed, the bankrupt homeowner may attempt to sell his home under the authority of the bankruptcy court or the bankruptcy trustee legally obligated to monitor the debtor's estate during the period of bankruptcy. Purchasing a home from a seller in bankruptcy entails more in the way of procedure and paperwork, but in general the specifics are the same as in an ordinary home purchase.

The seller in bankruptcy cannot unilaterally agree to the sale, but court approval or trustee approval must be obtained. The court or trustee generally looks to see if any proceeds from the sale can be distributed to the debtor's other creditors and, if such is the case, approves the sale. Accordingly, most purchase agreements between buyers and bankrupt sellers contain this clause: "Seller's obligations herein subject to bankruptcy court approval."

Listing agreements between bankrupt homeowners and real estate brokers are not uncommon and should not necessarily be shunned just because the seller happens to be in bankruptcy. Often, the buyer can obtain a somewhat better deal, due to the fact that the home must be sold quickly due to the bankrupt position of the debtor and the arrearages that undoubtedly exist on the current mortgage/loan.

HOMESTEAD EXEMPTION

Another means by which the homeowner may be able to protect his interest in the home is through the *homestead exemption* laws. These laws state that if the home is occupied by the homeowner and his family, an exemption that disallows any creditor to sell the home to satisfy a judgment for unsecured debts can be claimed. The majority of states have homestead exemption laws.

If the homeowner is faced with his home being sold for the aforementioned type of debts, a *declaration of homestead* must be filed with the applicable recorder's office to take advantage of the exemption. Without doing so, a judgment creditor may be able to force the sale of the home.

The amount of the homestead exemption is not unlimited. It is usually between $5,000 and $15,000 and, accordingly, only allows the homeowner a certain amount of limited protection.

Thus, if there exists a $10,000 homestead exemption law, and the owner's home equity is $30,000, the homeowner still has $20,000 at risk to satisfy these types of judgments.

With some exceptions, to claim a homestead exemption, the homeowner must be the head of a family (although in a few states a single person will be eligible); the homeowner and his family must actually live in the residence for which the homestead exemption is being claimed (which means only one homestead exemption can be claimed on one piece of property at any given time); and the homeowner must in fact own the property, although sometimes a long-term rental lease will qualify.

The homeowner should always remember that only unsecured debts for which the creditor has obtained a judgment lien are subordinate to the homestead exemption amount. Not included in the homestead exemption laws are property taxes or income tax liens, or voluntarily pledged mortgages, deeds of trust, or other types of voluntarily given security interests.

DISPUTE RESOLUTION— COURTS AND LAWYERS

It is a lucky homeowner who is never involved in a legal proceeding, either defending himself or by bringing a formal legal action. However, during the course of home ownership, it is likely that such an event will occur.

Attorneys

Whenever a legal real estate dispute arises, the homeowner must determine initially whether or not to obtain formal legal counsel to promote or defend his interests. The rule of thumb can be as follows: the more complex the issue, or the more money potentially at risk, the more likely it is that an attorney should be obtained.

In most cases, real estate attorneys charge on an hourly basis, but in some circumstances they may base their fee on a contingent basis. For instance, if faced with an eminent domain proceeding, and the government is offering the owner substantially less than what he believes the property is worth, an attorney may agree to be compensated pursuant to a percentage of the amount eventually received. This is called a *contingency fee agreement*.

Another good rule of practice with regard to attorneys is that if your opponent has obtained an attorney, you should obtain one also so as to proceed on an even playing field.

Small Claims or People's Court Every jurisdiction has a court in which individuals may present their claims without the assistance of attorneys. In fact, most of these *small claims* or *people's courts* specifically disallow attorneys.

Only certain types of claims can typically be heard in these courts. The local clerk of court's office can provide specific advice as to whether or not a certain claim may be heard in that court.

A potential disadvantage of small claims courts is that they usually place a limit on the amount of money in controversy. The party bringing the lawsuit may only be able to obtain a judgment for a certain amount and no more. If your claim is for more than the jurisdictional limit of the small claims court allows, you must either go to a court of higher jurisdiction or be satisfied with the limit the court can award.

Arbitration Arbitration is a device that can be used as an alternative by parties involved in a legal dispute so as to minimize costs, time, and attorney fees.

As mentioned in the chapter dealing with new construction and home remodeling projects, often the parties to a contract agree to take their dispute to arbitration. Arbitration is also available to parties involved in a legal dispute in the absence of a previously agreed upon contractual provision, if the parties later agree to submit their dispute to an arbitrator.

The local Better Business Bureau can often set up the arbitration hearing and will charge a fee for procuring the arbitrator to render a decision. The disadvantage to resolving disputes by arbitration is that if the parties do not abide by or comply with the decision, the arbitrator has little or no power of enforcement.

10

The Home as an Investment and Source of Income

Aside from being an integral part of the American dream, owning a home also has several long-term investment and income advantages.

INVESTMENT ADVANTAGES The home can be an attractive long-term economic investment. It can be used either as collateral for loans or as a device for increasing the homeowner's net worth.

Inflation Hedge Real estate has long been considered one of the best hedges against inflation. As the cost of living increases, so does the value of the home in most cases. Desirable residential living areas continue to be limited in availability due to the expanding population. This means that existing homes will, in all likelihood, be worth more than their original cost as the years and decades go by. Although this is a very broad and general statement, it has proven to be true during the better part of the century.

Also, as the value of the home increases, and the amount of the mortgage balance decreases, the homeowner is in effect enjoying tax-free income since the increased value of the home is not taxed. Even if the home is sold at a substantial profit, the one-time rollover exemption of $125,000 (as discussed in Chapter 7) can be used to avoid tax liability even if another home is not purchased.

A home also creates a forced savings aspect for the homeowner. As the homeowner periodically pays on the home loan, he is reducing his debt and simultaneously creating a long-term savings device due to the constantly increasing equity and value of the home.

Tax Advantages Several aspects of the inherent economic overhead involved in maintaining a residence are deductible from the homeowner's adjusted gross income. These include property taxes, interest on loans secured by the home, certain types of utility bills and charges thereon, home deductibility elements, and various conservation and energy improvements. These tax advantages of home ownership proportionately decrease the net cost of home ownership.

Inheritance Depending on how the title to the property is held, homeowners are also able to make sure that the home is passed on to family members. Different devices are available in this regard, including titling the home with the homeowner's children named as joint tenants; making sure the home is not sold but transferred intact pursuant to the terms of the homeowner's will; or various types of trust devices. This *legacy* aspect of owning a home is important to many homeowners and is an effective method of providing for the homeowner's heirs.

INVESTMENT DISADVANTAGES

Not all aspects of home ownership are economically advantageous. Certain relative disadvantages are involved.

Non-Liquidity A home's equity is the difference between any mortgage or security interest against the property and the market value of the home. As already mentioned, the homeowner is usually able to increase his equity in the home as time goes by. However, this is not the same thing as having ready access to cash. Thus, a homeowner can be "house rich" but "cash poor" due to the amount of money tied up in the home.

Some individuals who own their homes free and clear, but are limited to a set amount of money each month, such as Social Security or pension benefits, cannot take full advantage of the equity in their home. Of course, the homeowner may always sell his home to realize his equity, but he would still require suitable housing.

Certain lenders, however, now offer *reverse mortgage home equity lines of credit*. The "house rich" homeowner is able to borrow money against a pre-established line of credit and obtain funds as they are needed. No repayments are made; rather, the lender receives its money and accumulated interest when the house is eventually sold or transferred, often at the time of the borrower's death.

Deflation The previous section mentioned that home ownership is valuable as an inflation hedge. However, there have been certain periods of time when home values have gone down. This becomes critical to the homeowner who may be in the position of having to sell his home during one of these deflationary cycles, as he may receive less than was originally paid for the home and consequently owe more on the existing mortgage than what is realized on the sale.

There exists no current tax advantage or break to the homeowner who suffers such a loss. The perpetual increase of a home's value is never guaranteed, and this factor should be considered if contemplating a home purchase as an investment.

Home Maintenance   As may be overly obvious, there are periodic upkeep costs attendant with any long-term ownership of property, including a home.

Aside from the standard costs of mortgage loan payments, property taxes, and insurance on the home, the homeowner must also consider both annual and periodic update items, such as lawn maintenance, repainting, uninsured casualty losses, and so on.

Although these types of expenses are not always thought of by a potential first-time home buyer, they are necessary upkeep items that should be considered when determining if the home will be a wise investment or an economic yoke around the owner's neck.

Property Taxes   As mentioned before, one of the tax advantages of owning a home is that property taxes are 100 percent deductible on the adjustable gross income of the owner. One of the downsides of having to pay annual real estate taxes, however, is that they rarely decrease but often increase. Hence, since real estate taxes are usually included in the homeowner's monthly mortgage payment, more often than not the monthly payment will increase as property taxes rise.

INCOME SOURCES   As was reviewed in Chapter 7, the equity in the home can be used as collateral for many types of interest deductible loans, both oriented to improving the home (major remodeling projects) and loans for other types of necessities (as in a home equity loan), such as college tuition or medical bills. Other ways to utilize the home as a source of income are discussed here.

Lease with an Option to Buy   Also as discussed in Chapter 7, a homeowner may wish to enter into a lease with option to purchase. If the homeowner is required to move out of his home before it is sold, he may be able to lease out the home to offset the cost of the mortgage loan payment during the time he no longer occupies the home.

Home Office Tax Advantages   The advantage of the homeowner working out of his home can be substantial with regard to taxes. Since certain specific items may be deducted and depreciated for the dual use of the home as a business, the economic advantage is self-evident. Please see Chapter 7 for the specific advantages of the home office.

Refinancing   As lower interest rates become available, the homeowner may wish to refinance the loan on his home. This entails entering into a new mortgage and paying off the existing mortgage to lower the monthly payments based on the lower interest rate charged by the lender.

This element of control over the interest rate of the loan is another method that the homeowner can use to realize income. By lowering the amount of the monthly payment, the homeowner retains more money that would otherwise go to his mortgage loan payment based on the previous higher rate of interest.

Of course, the homeowner should only refinance if the inherent additional costs of refinancing the loan are outweighed by the amount of potential savings. The general rule is to refinance a home loan mortgage if a reduction of interest rates of two percent or more is available, taking into consideration how long the homeowner will be living in the home.

For example, it would not make sense for the homeowner to pay $1,000 in closing costs and discount points to refinance the home loan if he were only going to realize a monthly payment savings of $50, and if the owner planned to sell the home in the next twelve to eighteen months.

A homeowner who is going through the refinancing process should be aware that the Real Estate Settlement Procedures Act and Truth in Lending requirements that are involved in procuring a new loan do not come into play when refinancing. Since these disclosure laws under RESPA are not required when refinancing, the homeowner must make extra sure that all charges are justifiable and that no otherwise illegal or fraudulent activity has occurred. Please refer to Chapter 4 for a complete description of RESPA.

Sometimes the homeowner refinances at a different rate with regard to the length of the loan period. That is, if interest rates have dropped substantially, the homeowner may wish to reduce the length of his loan term from thirty to fifteen years.

The monthly payment may not decrease because of the lesser amount of time to repay the loan, and in fact may increase. However, if the new loan is paid off in fifteen years rather than the remaining portion of the thirty-year mortgage, after fifteen years the homeowner will have completed the home loan repayment process and be able to use that money in other ways.

CONCLUSION

I hope that the foregoing information proves helpful to anyone thinking of buying or selling a home, as well as anyone seeking to maximize his interests as a homeowner. Although the laws of residential real estate are often complex, they are outweighed by the simple satisfaction of owning your own home. Be it ever so humble ...

Glossary

ABSTRACT—A summary or digest of the conveyances, transfers, and any other documents relied upon as evidence of title, including elements of public record that may affect the marketability of the title to the home.

ACCELERATION CLAUSE—A provision in the deed of trust or mortgage giving the lender the right to declare all sums owing it to be immediately due and payable upon the happening of a certain event, usually the sale or transfer of the home.

ACKNOWLEDGMENT OF POWER OF SALE—A document signed by the borrower acknowledging that the security given for the loan is a deed of trust and that its enforcement provisions are different from a mortgage.

ACTUAL NOTICE—The type of notice or information that is brought directly to the attention of an individual, usually by means of firsthand knowledge or observation.

ADDENDUM—A document that is added to or supplemental to an original contract; usually used to clarify or add to the original terms of the contract.

ADJUSTABLE RATE MORTGAGE—A mortgage containing a provision that specifically provides that the interest rate charged by the lender will increase (or decrease) periodically.

ADVERSE POSSESSION—The acquiring of title to real estate by means of unauthorized occupancy of the property for a period of time established by law.

AGENCY RELATIONSHIP—The legal relationship in which one party acts on behalf of another in dealing with third parties; the individual who acts on behalf of another is termed the agent, while the individual for whom the agent acts is termed the principal.

APPRAISAL—An estimate and formal opinion of value of a particular parcel of real estate.

ASSIGNMENT OF LEASEHOLD INTEREST—A transfer to another of all rights and obligations to an interest in real estate, typically with regard to the transfer of landlord rights and obligations from a seller to a buyer of real estate being utilized as rental property.

ATTESTATION—The act of witnessing the execution of a written document and subscribing said document as a witness.

ATTORNEY'S OPINION—An opinion furnished by an attorney with regard to the marketability or validity of title to a particular parcel of real estate, typically used when the buyer requires some assurance of title from the seller prior to closing.

BALLOON PAYMENT—The final payment of principal under a promissory note that contains a provision requiring a substantial payment of principal at the end of the repayment term.

BARGAIN AND SALE DEED—A type of deed that conveys title but makes no warranties with regard to the condition of the title to the property being transferred.

BENEFICIARY—The lender in a deed of trust loan.

BINDER — A written commitment by a title insurance company stating that a title insurance policy will be issued to the home buyer if and when said buyer takes title to the property.

BLANKET MORTGAGE—A mortgage that covers or utilizes two or more parcels of real estate, which are pledged as security for the debt.

BREACH OF CONTRACT—Failure, without legal excuse or justification, to perform any promise or condition of a contract.

BUYER'S BROKER—A real estate broker who acts as the legal authorized agent for a potential home buyer.

BUYER'S QUESTION RULE—A rule of real estate sale disclosure mandating that the seller or seller's broker must not only truthfully answer any questions that the buyer has with regard to the condition of the property, but must also notify the buyer of any subsequent change in said condition.

BY-LAWS—The adopted self-governing rules of a corporation.

CAP—The maximum amount that a lender can increase the interest rate and/or amount of monthly payment of a mortgage utilized in an adjustable rate loan.

CASH FOR DEED—A real estate purchase in which the buyer pays the seller the agreed upon sale price in full at the time of closing in exchange for the deed to the property.

CAVEAT EMPTOR—Latin phrase meaning "let the buyer beware."

CERTIFICATE OF OCCUPANCY—The document issued by a local governing body indicating that the newly constructed building has met all building code regulations and is legally certified as safe for occupancy.

CHAIN OF TITLE—A series of successive conveyances indicating previous owners and individuals who have had interest in a specific piece of real estate.

CLOSING SECRETARY—The individual who conducts the closing of the sale of real estate, typically on behalf of the lender or listing broker.

CLOUD ON TITLE—An outstanding claim or encumbrance, which, if valid, affects or impairs the title to a particular piece of real estate.

COMMINGLING OF FUNDS—The act of an agent in mingling his money with the money entrusted to him, which is to be held on his principal's behalf; said act generally considered to be a breach of the agent's duty to his principal.

COMMITMENT PERIOD—The time between the issuance of a title insurance binder and the issuance of a title insurance policy; may also be the period between when a lender agrees to make a loan to a particular borrower and the time that the loan is actually received by the borrower.

CONDEMNATION PROCEEDING—The procedure whereby a privately owned parcel of real estate is taken and transferred to a governmental entity under the power of eminent domain.

CONSIDERATION—The act or promise bargained for and transferred in exchange for another act or promise; a necessary element for a contractual agreement to exist.

CONSTRUCTION LIEN—A lien obtained by an individual who furnishes work, labor, or materials for the permanent improvement of real estate; also known as a mechanic's lien.

CONSTRUCTION MORTGAGE—A loan in which the lender periodically advances money to a buyer building a new home, with the money being advanced as needed by the builder; the security for the loan is the home being built.

CONSTRUCTIVE NOTICE—The type of legal note that is implied or imputed by law, as in the case of documents that have been recorded in the appropriate public registry.

CONTINGENCY FEE AGREEMENT—A type of fee arrangement, typically used between home sellers and real estate brokers, whereby the real estate broker only receives a fee for his services if and when the property is sold.

COOPERATIVE BROKER—A real estate broker who has no listing agreement with a home seller, but nevertheless represents the seller as a sub-broker of the seller and assists the buyer in searching for and purchasing a home.

CORPORATE RESOLUTION—A document drafted and executed by appropriate corporate officers authorizing or ratifying an act or contract entered into by the corporation.

COUNTER OFFER—A response to an offer, which changes one or more of the terms or conditions of the original offer.

COVENANT AGAINST ENCUMBRANCES—An implied promise contained within a warranty deed, providing that there are no encumbrances, mortgages, or liens on the property except those that are stated in the deed, or are a matter of public record, or are otherwise made known to the buyer.

COVENANT OF QUIET ENJOYMENT—An implied promise contained within a warranty deed that provides that the buyer will not be removed or disturbed in his enjoyment or possession of the home by anyone having paramount title.

COVENANT OF SEISIN—An implied promise contained within a warranty deed, providing that the grantor has the legal right and authority to convey the home.

CREDIT DEFECTS—An aspect of a potential borrower's credit or economic history that dissuades a lender from granting the loan as applied for.

DEED—A written document used to convey real estate.

DEED IN LIEU OF FORECLOSURE—A deed transferred from a homeowner to a lender to prevent the lender from proceeding or commencing with a foreclosure action.

DEED OF TRUST—A deed transferred by a home buyer by which title of the home is placed in the name of a trustee to secure repayment of a loan; a security device utilized by lenders making loans for home purchases.

DEFICIENCY BALANCE—The money owed from a borrower to a lender subsequent to a mortgage foreclosure action, in which the amount realized from the foreclosure sale is less than the total balance owed.

DISCOUNT POINTS—Additional charges made by a lender at the time the loan is made; the amount of a point is equal to one percent (1%) of the loan amount and is used to increase the rate of return to the lender so as to approximate the market level of prevailing interest rates.

DOWER—The potential interest that one spouse has in the other spouse's real estate ownership.

DUE ON SALE CLAUSE—A condition contained in a mortgage or deed of trust, requiring the borrower to pay off the loan balance if the property is transferred or sold.

EARNEST MONEY DEPOSIT—The money used as a down payment by the buyer of real estate as evidence of good faith and serious intention; usually forwarded to the seller at the time the purchase offer is made and credited to the buyer at the time of closing.

EASEMENT—A non-possessory interest in real estate that allows an individual to use another's property for a limited or pre-designated purpose.

EMINENT DOMAIN—The power to take private property for public use by the government; entails the obligation to reimburse the owner the fair value of the property taken.

ENCROACHMENT—An illegal or unauthorized intrusion by one property owner onto the property of another, usually by way of a misplaced wall, fence, or shrub.

ENCUMBRANCE—Any right to or interest in real estate that may detract or reduce the interest of the owner of the property; a claim, lien, or liability that has been attached to real estate to the detriment of the owner.

EQUITABLE INTEREST—The interest in real estate that a buyer has during the life of a land installment sales contract.

ESCROW ACCOUNT—An account or depository of funds that is used by an agent to hold or retain money of his principal or another third party.

ESTOPPEL CERTIFICATE—A document signed by a borrower stating that, if he should default on his mortgage or deed of trust, he waives any potential legal defenses to any action that the lender may take to enforce its interest.

EVIDENCE OF TITLE—Any means or evidence satisfactory to a buyer of real estate indicating that the seller has good and sufficient title and is able to transfer ownership; typically a title insurance policy or an attorney's opinion is utilized to establish evidence of title.

EXCLUSIVE AGENCY LISTING—A contract between a real estate broker and a homeowner, giving the broker sole authority to sell the home to the exclusion of all other real estate brokers; the homeowner retains the right to sell the home independent of the broker without becoming liable for a commission.

EXCLUSIVE RIGHT TO SELL LISTING—A contract between a real estate broker and a homeowner, giving the broker sole authority to sell the home to the exclusion of all other real estate brokers; the broker is entitled to a commission even if the home is sold solely through the homeowner's efforts.

EXECUTOR—The individual or entity charged with carrying out the terms of a will or an estate; also known as Personal Representative.

FEE SIMPLE ABSOLUTE—An extensive ownership interest in real estate; an ownership interest that is potentially indefinite in duration.

FIDUCIARY DUTY—The legal duty owed from an agent to a principal pursuant to an agency relationship, in which the agent is legally obligated to promote and protect his principal's interests.

FIXED RATE LOAN—A loan in which the interest rate charged does not change over the life of the loan, regardless of any interest rate changes in the prevailing economic market.

FIXTURE—An item of personal property that is permanently attached to real estate and, by means of said attachment, is legally considered part of the real estate.

FLOAT — The process in which a loan applicant agrees to be charged whatever interest rate is currently available in the market, as determined by the lender, at the time the loan is made, as opposed to the time the loan application is made.

FOR SALE BY OWNER—The sale or attempted sale of real estate without the professional assistance of a real estate broker.

FORECLOSURE—The legal process by which a mortgagor obtains a foreclosure decree and the forced sale of the property used as security for the loan.

FORECLOSURE SALE—The forced sale of mortgaged property to allow the mortgagor to recoup the balance of a loan secured by the property being sold.

FSBO—An abbreviation of For Sale By Owner.

FUTURE ADVANCEMENTS—The phrased utilized in an open end mortgage that allows the borrower to borrow additional funds, usually at the original interest rate; often the maximum amount available is limited to the original amount borrowed.

GENERAL POWER OF ATTORNEY — An instrument authorizing another to act as one's agent or representative, including the power to sell or purchase real estate.

GRANTEE—The person or entity who receives real estate, usually by way of deed.

GRANTOR—The person or entity who transfers real estate to another, usually by way of a deed.

HOMESTEAD EXEMPTION — The laws that exempt a certain portion of the family home from a forced sale by certain classes of creditors.

IMPLIED WARRANTY—A promise or guarantee arising by operation of law that the product sold or transferred is merchantable and fit for the purpose for which it was built or designed.

INDEMNIFICATION—To restore or repay the victim of a loss, in whole or in part, by payment, repair, or replacement.

INDEPENDENT CONTRACTOR—An individual or entity who, in the exercise of an independent employment agreement, contracts to do work or achieve a particular result and is only responsible for the end product or final result; not considered an employee.

INSTALLMENT LAND CONTRACT — A real estate purchase agreement in which the buyer makes periodic payments to the seller over an extended period of time rather than paying the entire purchase price at the time of closing.

JOINT TENANCY — A form of co-ownership of real estate in which the entire property passes to the surviving joint tenant upon the death of the other joint tenant or tenants.

JUDGMENT LIEN—An interest in real estate obtained by a creditor who has obtained a judgment against the property owner.

JUDGMENT SALE—The sale of real estate pursuant to a judgment entered against the homeowner, usually conducted by the sheriff or local judicial authorities.

LATENT DEFECT—A type of defect in real estate that materially affects the value of a home and is not readily apparent to the buyer.

LEGAL DESCRIPTION—A precise description of real estate by either a governmental survey or lot numbers of a recorded plat map.

LEGAL TITLE—The ownership interest of a seller in an installment land contract during the life of the contract.

LIEN—A security interest or an encumbrance on real estate.

LIEN WAIVER AFFIDAVIT—A document executed by the seller of real estate, indicating that no recent improvements to the property have occurred that may subsequently cause a construction lien to be placed on the property after it is transferred to a buyer.

LIFE ESTATE—A real estate interest that is of limited duration—either the life of the owner or a third party.

LIQUIDATED DAMAGES—An agreed upon specific sum to be awarded to a damaged party if a breach of contract occurs.

LIS PENDENS—Written public notice that a pending lawsuit exists, which may affect title or ownership rights to certain real estate.

LISTING BROKER—A real estate broker who has entered into a listing agreement with a homeowner for the sale of the home.

LOCKING IN—The method of a borrower in securing or obtaining a guaranteed specific interest rate for a set period of time between the time of loan commitment and closing.

MATERIAL DEFECTS—Any defect in real estate that substantially affects the value of the property or the owner's use of the property.

MECHANIC'S LIEN—See CONSTRUCTION LIEN.

METES AND BOUNDS—A method or type of legal description utilizing boundary lines of lands, with various terminal points and angles.

MITIGATE DAMAGES—The duty or ability to otherwise reduce one's damages pursuant to a breach of contract; a necessary prerequisite to maintaining a cause of action for breach of contract.

MORTGAGE—The document granting an interest in real estate from the borrower to the lender as security for the loan.

MORTGAGE FORECLOSURE SALE—See FORECLOSURE SALE.

MORTGAGEE—The lender that receives the loan payments from the borrower.

MORTGAGOR—The borrower who grants the lender a mortgage as security for the loan.

NEGATIVE AMORTIZATION — An increase in a borrower's mortgage balance due to the existence of a payment cap limitation but not an interest rate cap limitation, thus preventing the periodic payment from covering the entire principal owed for that particular payment.

NEGATIVE FRAUD—Failure by a home seller to disclose material defects in the property to a potential buyer.

NEGLIGENCE—The failure of an individual to use such care as a reasonably prudent person would use under similar circumstances.

NEGLIGENT MISREPRESENTATION—Similar to NEGATIVE FRAUD; the failure of the duty of a home seller to disclose to a potential buyer material defects that affect the use or condition of the home.

NON-EXCLUSIVE LISTING—A contract between a real estate broker and a homeowner whereby the real estate broker attempts to sell the home on behalf of the owner for a predetermined price. The homeowner may simultaneously enter into several non-exclusive listing agreements without regard to the number of brokers who may be attempting to sell the house; only the broker who procures a buyer receives the agreed upon commission. Also known as an open listing.

NOTICE OF DEFAULT—Formal notification by a lender to a borrower that the borrower has violated one or more terms of the loan and mortgage.

OFFER—A proposal by a potential real estate buyer intended to create a binding purchase agreement if the offer is accepted unconditionally by the seller.

OPEN END MORTGAGE—A loan and mortgage in which the borrower is allowed to procure additional funds from the lender, usually up to the initial amount borrowed, under the same security agreement and typically at the original interest rate.

OPEN LISTING—See NON-EXCLUSIVE LISTING.

OPTION TO PURCHASE—A real estate contract between a seller and potential buyer in which the buyer pays for the right to possibly purchase the property within a certain period of time allotted.

PACKAGE MORTGAGE—A type of loan in which security for the loan is both real estate and personal property.

PAR RATE—The rate of interest charged by a lender without the added charge of discount points.

PATENT DEFECT—A type of material defect in real estate that is obvious or apparent to a lay person; typically discovered by firsthand observation.

PERSONAL REPRESENTATIVE—See EXECUTOR.

POWER OF SALE—The authority given to a trustee under a deed of trust in which the trustee is allowed to proceed with the sale of the property used as security for a loan upon breach of the terms of the loan by the borrower.

PRE-QUALIFIED—A potential buyer of real estate that has already obtained loan approval for the amount necessary to purchase the home involved.

PROMISSORY NOTE—The document setting forth the terms of a loan.

PURCHASE MONEY MORTGAGE—A mortgage or security device received by the seller from the buyer of real estate to secure a loan made by the seller to the buyer, which allows the purchase to occur.

QUITCLAIM DEED—A type of deed that only conveys whatever title the grantor may have, if any.

REAFFIRMATION AGREEMENT—An agreement entered into between a homeowner and a lender in which the homeowner agrees to continue with the loan payments, despite the homeowner's filing of bankruptcy.

RELEASE OF LIEN—A document signed by a lien holder releasing any interest that individual or entity may have in the property; usually used in conjunction with a previously filed construction lien or judgment lien.

RESCIND—To legally cancel an otherwise binding contract.

RESTRICTIVE COVENANT—A private agreement that restricts or controls the use or condition of real estate.

RIGHT OF REDEMPTION — A homeowner's right to redeem ownership of his property subsequent to a foreclosure decree; usually contingent upon the homeowner paying all arrearages to the lender.

RIGHT OF SURVIVORSHIP—An inherent right of owners of real estate held by joint tenancy; the surviving joint tenant or tenants continue to own the property while the interest of the deceased joint tenant does not pass to his heirs.

ROLLOVER MORTGAGE—A type of loan that is mandatorily renegotiated on a periodic basis so as to allow the lender to increase the interest rate charged.

RUN WITH THE LAND—Any type of prohibition or use restriction on real estate that continues to exist despite any subsequent transfer of ownership.

SATISFACTION OF JUDGMENT—A document filed by a judgment creditor, indicating that the judgment balance owed by the homeowner has been paid in full.

SECURITY INTEREST—An interest in real estate obtained by a lender as security for a loan made to the property owner.

SETTLEMENT CLERK—See CLOSING SECRETARY.

SITUATIONAL SURVEY—The process of surveying land to ascertain its specific boundaries and guaranteeing said boundaries to the owner of the property.

SPECIFIC PERFORMANCE—A legal remedy in which the potential buyer of real estate requests that the court require the seller to abide by the terms of a purchase agreement and transfer the property to the buyer as contracted.

STATUTE OF FRAUDS—A body of law requiring that certain contracts, including real estate purchase agreements, be in writing to be enforceable.

SUB-BROKER—See COOPERATIVE BROKER.

TAX SALE—The forced sale of real estate pursuant to the nonpayment of real estate taxes or income taxes.

TENANCY BY THE ENTIRETY—The co-ownership of real estate between spouses, with the survivor remaining as the sole owner.

TENANCY IN COMMON—A form of concurrent ownership of real estate in which each owner possesses an undivided right to the entire parcel of property, with each owner's right similar to those possessed by a sole owner; no right of survivorship exists.

THEORY OF NON-CONFORMING USE—The legal theory that allows an owner of real estate not to be bound by applicable zoning law restrictions due to the owner's use of the property prior to the enactment of the zoning laws.

TITLE—Ownership rights to real estate.

TITLE DEFECT—Real estate ownership that has a particular defect or negative interest against the property owner, which may affect the transferability rights of the owner.

TITLE INSURANCE—An insurance policy issued to protect any loss or damage that may result from defects of title to real estate.

TITLE INSURANCE BINDER—See BINDER.

TITLE SEARCH—The review of public records to determine the status of ownership and potential third party interests or claims with regard to a particular piece of real estate.

TRUSTEE—The individual or entity who, pursuant to a deed of trust, is authorized to sell the real estate given as security for a loan, should the buyer default.

TRUSTOR—The individual who is borrowing money from the lender and is giving a deed of trust to the trustee as security for the loan.

UNIFORM SETTLEMENT STATEMENT—A form settlement statement that contains a summary of the buyer's and seller's closing transaction, including an itemization of all settlement charges at closing.

VA/FHA ESCAPE CLAUSE—A provision in a real estate purchase agreement involving the VA or FHA whereby if the appraisal of the home is less than the purchase price, the buyer is not obligated to purchase the home and is entitled to the full return of his earnest deposit.

VARIABLE RATE MORTGAGE—A mortgage loan that contains a provision permitting the lender to periodically increase or decrease the interest rate charged in a manner specified in the mortgage.

VARIANCE—Permission given to an owner of real estate so as to use the property differently than required by the zoning laws.

WALK-THROUGH—The on-site inspection of a home by a buyer immediately preceding the closing so as to determine that the property is in the same condition as when the purchase agreement was signed.

WARRANTY DEED—A type of deed that contains within it certain implied covenants or promises that provide the buyer with various remedies in the event that the transfer of property or ownership rights in the property is not total and complete.

ZONE CHANGE—The process of obtaining a different classification for the area in which real estate may be located so as to change the available utilization of the property.

Appendices

LISTING CONTRACT

_____, Nebraska

_____, 19_____

IN CONSIDERATION of your agreement to list, and to offer for sale the property hereinafter described and to use your efforts to find a purchaser, I hereby give you the sole and exclusive right until _____ to sell _____

for the sum of _____ (_____) dollars, and upon the following terms _____ _____.

I agree to pay you a cash commission of _____ per cent of the gross sale price, said commission to be payable on the happening of any one or more of the following events, to wit:

If a sale is made, or a purchaser found, who is ready, willing and able to purchase the property before the expiration of this listing, by you, myself, or any other person, at the above price and terms or for any other price and terms I may agree to accept, or if this agreement is revoked or violated by me, or if you are prevented in closing the sale of this property by existing liens, judgments, or suits pending against this property, or the owners thereof, or if you are unfairly hindered by me in the showing of, or advertising to sell said premises, within the stated period, or if within three months after the expiration of this listing I make a sale of said premises to anyone due to your efforts or advertising done under this listing.

I hereby represent that to the best of my knowledge, information and belief there are no termites in the buildings on the real estate herinbefore described, and if termites are found in said buildings and it is known that such condition existed prior to the date of the closing of the sale thereof, I hereby agree to indemnify you and hold you harmless from any or all costs, damage or expenses to which you may be subjected arising in connection therewith.

In case of forfeiture, by a prospective purchaser, of any earnest money payment, upon the within described property, said earnest money, after expenses incurred by the agent have been deducted, shall be divided equally between the parties hereto, in proportion of one-half to the owner and one-half to the agent; Provided, that in no event shall the agents share exceed the amount of the commission provided for in this contract.

In the event of sale, I agree to, without delay, furnish title insurance or a complete abstract, certified to date, showing good and merchantable title and to pay any expense incurred in perfecting the title in case same is found defective, and convey the property within _____ from date of sale, by warranty deed or _____ executed by all persons having any interest therein, clear of all encumbrances except _____ _____

which encumbrances if assumed by the purchaser, shall be part of the agreed purchase price.

You are authorized to place a "For Sale" sign on the above property.

I agree to give possession within _____ from the date of closing.

_____
_____
Owners

We accept the above listing and agree to the terms thereof on this day and date above written.

_____
Agent

The owner acknowledges receipt of a copy of this listing contract as of the above written date.

_____
_____
Owners

(This is a legally binding contract. If not understood, seek legal advice.)

PURCHASE AGREEMENT

This form is acceptable to the Nebraska Real Estate Commission

...., Agent

...., Nebraska ...., 19......

I, the undersigned Purchaser, hereby agree to purchase the property described as follows:

Address .... Legal Description ....

.... including all fixtures and equipment permanently attached to said premises. The only personal property included is as follows: ....

Subject, however, and on condition that the owner thereof has good, valid and marketable title, in fee simple, and said owner agrees to convey title to said property to me or my nominees by warranty deed .... free and clear of all liens, encumbrances or special taxes levied or assessed, except ....

I agree to pay for same... ($..................) DOLLARS, on the following terms: $.................. deposited herewith as evidenced by your receipt attached below. Balance to be paid as shown in Paragraph(s) # .... following, which paragraph(s) numbered 1 to 5 inclusive as being applicable to this agreement.

#1 Balance of $.................. to be paid in cash or by certified check at time of delivery of deed, no financing
All Cash being required.

#2 Balance of $.................. to be paid in cash or by certified check at time of delivery of deed, conditional
Conditional however, upon my ability to obtain a loan to be secured by first mortgage on above described property, in the
Upon Loan amount of $.................. Said loan to be VA.................., FHA (Farmers Home Administration)

.................., FHA (Federal Housing Administration) ...., CONVENTIONAL ....

M.G.I.C. ...., or VA/FHA ...., with terms providing for interest not exceeding ....%

per annum, and monthly payments of approximately $.......... plus taxes and insurance. I agree to make application for said loan immediately upon acceptance of this offer. I hereby authorize you to negotiate for a loan on the above basis, and I agree to sign all papers and pay all costs in connection therewith, and to establish escrow reserves as required. If said loan is not approved within .... days from date of acceptance hereof, this offer to be null and void, and the money paid herewith to be returned to me. Provided, however, that if processing of the application has not been completed by the lending agency within the above time, such time limit shall be automatically extended until the lending agency has in the normal course of its business advised either approval or rejection.

#3

Assume Existing Mortgage

I agree to assume and pay existing mortgage balance in favor of .... in the approximate amount of $.................. and pay the balance in cash or by certified check at time of delivery of deed; it being understood that present mortgage terms call for interest rate of ....% per annum and payments of $.................. per .... Said payment includes ....

Interest on existing loan to be prorated to date of closing. I also agree to reimburse the Seller for the amount in the escrow reserve account which is to be assigned to me.

#4

Land Contract

Balance to be evidenced by land contract with present owner, providing for additional cash payment or certified check of $.................. at time of execution of the contract, and remainder of $.................. to be paid in monthly payments of $.................., or more, which monthly payments shall include interest at the rate of ....% per annum computed monthly on the unpaid portion of the principal.

#5

.... (over)

Possession of said premises shall be delivered to me on or before ....

Seller (Sellers) shall pay all taxes to and including .... Taxes for the year ....

.... together with interest and rents, if any, shall be prorated to date of possession.

It is understood and agreed that in the event sellers hold title to said property as joint tenants, they are contracting as joint tenants in their acceptance of this offer.

Seller agrees to furnish within fifteen (15) days from date of the acceptance of this offer a complete abstract of title, certified to date by a bonded abstractor, or a title insurance commitment (binder). Purchaser agrees to deliver to Seller within ten (10) days thereafter a copy of attorney's opinion showing defects, if any, in said title. In the event Purchaser's attorney finds defects in said title, Seller, after written notice thereof, shall endeavor to have the same cured to the satisfaction of Purchaser within a reasonable time after the receipt of notice thereof, and if not so cured within said time, then either Purchaser or Seller may rescind this agreement, whereupon Seller shall then refund to Purchaser the deposit made hereunder. Purchaser agrees to close said purchase within .... days after delivery of said abstract of title or title commitment, or in the event defects are found in said title, within ten (10) days after such defects are cured. The cost of any title insurance policy issued in connection with this sale shall be equally divided between Purchaser and Seller. It is understood that the documentary revenue on the conveyance is to be paid for by Seller.

This offer is based upon my personal inspection or investigation of the premises and not upon any representation or warranties of condition by the Seller or his agent. Seller agrees to maintain, until delivery of possession, the heating, air conditioning, water heater, sewer, plumbing and electrical systems and any built-in appliances in working condition.

It is understood and agreed that this agreement shall in no manner be construed to convey title to said property or to give any right to take possession thereof.

It is understood and agreed that both parties retain their right to bring action for Specific Performance in the event the other party is in default in carrying out his obligations under this contract.

Any risk of loss to the property shall be borne by the Seller until title has been conveyed to the Purchaser. In the event prior to closing the structures on said property are materially damaged by fire, explosion or any other cause, Purchaser shall have the right to rescind this agreement, whereupon Seller shall then refund to Purchaser the deposit made hereunder. Purchaser agrees to pay the cost of a termite inspection of the house and attached structures, and Seller agrees to pay for any treatment or repair work found necessary.

WITNESS:

...., **Purchaser**

...., **Purchaser**

Address.. Phone..................

RECEIVED FROM ....

the sum of .... ($....................) DOLLARS
to apply on the purchase price of the above described property on terms and conditions as stated herein, it being hereby agreed and understood that in the event the above offer is not accepted by the owner of said property within the time hereinafter specified, or that in the event there are any defects in the title which cannot be cured as specified above, the money hereby paid is to be refunded. In the event of refusal or failure of the Purchaser to consummate the purchase, the owner may at his option, retain the said money hereby paid, as liquidated damages for such failure to carry out said agreement of sale.

This receipt is not an acceptance of the above offer, it being understood that the above proposition is taken subject to the written approval and acceptance by the owner on or before ....

...., Agent

By...

#5..

ACCEPTANCE

...., Nebraska ....

.... 19 ....

...., hereby accept the foregoing proposition on the terms stated and agree to convey title to said property, deliver possession and perform all the terms and conditions set forth.

.... further agree to pay to the named Agent $................... cash for professional services.

....

....
Seller

WITNESS:

....

STATE OF NEBRASKA }
COUNTY OF .... } ss.

On this .... day of ...., A.D. 19 ...., before me .... a Notary Public in and for said county, personally came ....

....

....

to me personally known to be the identical person... whose name .... affixed to the within instrument as owner .... and .... acknowledged the execution of the same to be .... voluntary act and deed for the purpose therein expressed.

IN WITNESS WHEREOF, I have hereunto subscribed my name and affixed my seal at ...., Nebraska, on the day last above written.

....
Notary Public

PURCHASER PLEASE NOTE

In closing your purchase, we, as agents, are required to have cash, or its equivalent, upon conveyance of title. Please bring cash, certified check or cashier's check for the balance of your payment. This will permit us to deliver papers promptly.

SELLER PLEASE NOTE

Upon termination of Seller's insurance at closing, Seller should insure all personal property remaining on the premises prior to delivering possession.

Note: While this form is acceptable to the Nebraska Real Estate Commission, its use is not mandatory and it will not be suitable for contracts having unusual provisions.

KNOW ALL MEN BY THESE PRESENTS:

That

of the   County of   , and State of
for the consideration of the sum of   DOLLARS
in hand paid, at or before the ensealing and delivery of these presents by

of the   County of   , and State of
have agreed and do hereby agree to hold until the   day of   , 19
at 12 o'clock M., time being the essence and important part of this option, subject to the order of the said

, or assigns, the following described property, to-wit:

or to transfer the said property at any time within the time above prescribed, to the said

or such person or persons as he or they may direct at and

for the price of   DOLLARS

good and lawful money of the United States of America, payable on the following terms:

In the event that the holder or holders of this option shall decide to purchase the said property at the above price and terms within the said time, then and in that case, the said amount paid for this option shall be credited upon the said purchase price, but in the event the holder or holders hereof do not conclude the purchase above named within the time prescribed, then and in that case, the said amount paid for this option shall be retained by the undersigned in full satisfaction for holding the property subject to the said order for the said time.

It is provided, however, that in case there should be any delay on the part of the undersigned in perfecting the title to the above property for more than .... days after notice of the election of the holder or holders hereof to purchase the said property, then and in that case the holder or holders hereof reserves the right to cancel this option and receive back the consideration herefor or to extend the time until said title is perfected.

Dated at ....(Seal)

this............day of............................, 19.......... ....(Seal)

STATE OF ...., County of............................:

Before me, a notary public qualified for said county, personally came

.... known to me to be the identical person or persons who signed the foregoing instrument and acknowledged the execution thereof to be his, her or their voluntary act and deed.

Witness my hand and notarial seal on............................, 19..........

My commission expires............................, 19.......... ....Notary Public

STATE OF............................ ⎱
County of............................ ⎰ss.

Entered on numerical index and filed for record in the Register of Deeds Office of said County the ....day of............................, 19......., at............o'clock and............minutes............M.,

and recorded in Book............of............at page............

....Reg. of Deeds

By............................Deputy

REAL PROPERTY MORTGAGE

in consideration of

received from mortgagee, does mortgage to

, herein called the mortgagor whether one or more,

And the mortgagor does hereby covenant with the mortgagee and with mortgagee's heirs and assigns that mortgagor is lawfully seised of said premises, that they are free from encumbrance, that mortgagor has good right and lawful authority to convey the same, and that mortgagor warrants and will defend the title to said premises against the lawful claims of all persons whomsoever.

This mortgage is given to secure the payment of the promissory note of this date made by mortgagor for $ payable

Mortgagor shall pay all taxes and assessments levied upon said real property and all other taxes levied on this mortgage or the note which this mortgage is given to secure before the same become delinquent and shall maintain fire, windstorm and extended coverage insurance with a mortgage clause on the buildings on said premises in the sum of $ If mortgagor fails to pay such taxes and assessments or procure such insurance, mortgagee may pay such taxes and purchase such insurance and the amount so advanced with interest at nine percent per annum shall be secured by this mortgage. In case of default in the payment of the principal sum or any installment thereof or of any interest thereon when the same shall become due or in case of the non-payment of any taxes or assessments or of the failure to maintain insurance as herein provided, mortgagee may at the option of mortgagee, without notice, at any time during the continuance of such default or breach, declare the whole debt secured by this mortgage to be immediately due and payable and may foreclose this mortgage.

In the event of default in the performance of any of the terms and conditions of this mortgage or the note secured by it, the mortgagee shall be entitled to immediate possession of the property above described and all the rents, revenue and income derived therefrom during such time as the mortgage indebtedness remains unpaid shall be applied by the mortgagee to the payment of the note and all other sums secured hereby after deduction of any necessary costs of collection.

Dated .... 19 ....

....

STATE OF NEBRASKA, County of .... :

The foregoing instrument was acknowledged before me .... 19 ....

by ....

....
Signature of Person Taking Acknowledgment

....
Title

STATE OF NEBRASKA, County of .... :
Filed for record and entered in Numerical Index on
.... at .... o'clock .... M.,
and recorded in Mortgage Record ...., Page ....

.... By .... Deputy County Clerk or
County Clerk or   Deputy Register of Deeds
Register of Deeds

ACKNOWLEDGMENT OF POWER OF SALE

(To be signed prior to execution of Deed of Trust)

Property Address: _____

TO: _____

_____

STATE OF NEBRASKA   )
) SS

COUNTY OF _____   )

The undersigned, being first duly sworn on oath, state as follows:

1. The undersigned are or will be the borrower (whether one or more) under a certain loan from _____, and as security for such loan, the undersigned will execute and deliver a Deed of Trust covering the above described property to _____.

2. The undersigned understand and acknowledge that such securing instrument is a deed of trust and not a mortgage and that the power of sale contained in such deed of trust provides substantially different rights and obligations to the undersigned than a mortgage in an event of default or breach of obligation.

Dated: _____

                                             _____

                                             _____

SUBSCRIBED AND SWORN TO before me, a notary public in and for said county and state, this _____ day of _____, 19_____.

                                             _____
                                             Notary Public

(Seal)

DEED OF TRUST

THIS DEED OF TRUST, is made as of the _____ day of _____, 19____, by and among _____ ("Trustor"), whose mailing address is _____ ("Trustee"), whose mailing address is _____,

and _____ ("Beneficiary") whose mailing address is _____.

FOR VALUABLE CONSIDERATION, Trustor irrevocably transfers, conveys and assigns to Trustee, IN TRUST, WITH POWER OF SALE, for the benefit and security of Beneficiary, under and subject to the terms and conditions of this Deed of Trust, the real property located in the City of _____, County of _____, State of Nebraska, and legally described as follows (the "Property"):

TOGETHER WITH, all rents, easements, appurtenances, hereditaments, interests in adjoining roads, streets and alleys, improvements and buildings of any kind situated thereon and all personal property that may be or hereafter become an integral part of such buildings and improvements, all crops raised thereon, and all water rights.

The Property and the entire estate and interest conveyed to the Trustee are referred to collectively as the "Trust Estate".

FOR THE PURPOSE OF SECURING:

a. Payment of indebtness in the total principal amount of $ _____, with interest thereon, as evidenced by that certain promissory note of even date (the "Note") with a maturity date of _____, executed by Trustor, which has been delivered and is payable to the order of Beneficiary, and which by this reference is hereby made a part hereof, and any and all modifications, extensions and renewals thereof, and

b. Payment of all sums advanced by Beneficiary to protect the Trust Estate, with interest thereon at the rate of _____ percent (____%) per annum.

This Deed of Trust, the Note, and any other instrument given to evidence or further secure the payment and performance of any obligation secured hereby are referred to collectively as the "Loan Instruments".

TO PROTECT THE SECURITY OF THIS DEED OF TRUST:

1. PAYMENT OF INDEBTEDNESS. Trustor shall pay when due the principal of, and the interest on, the indebtedness evidenced by the Note, charges, fees and all other sums as provided in the Loan Instruments.

2. TAXES. Trustor shall pay each installment of all taxes and special assessments of every kind, now or hereafter levied against the Trust Estate or any part thereof, before delinquency, without notice or demand, and shall provide Beneficiary with evidence of the payment of same. Trustor shall pay all taxes and assessments which may be levied upon Beneficiary's interest herein or upon this Deed of Trust or the debt secured hereby, without regard to any law that may be enacted imposing payment of the whole or any part thereof upon the Beneficiary.

3. INSURANCE AND REPAIRS. Trustor shall maintain fire and not extended coverage insurance insuring the improvements and buildings constituting part of the Trust Estate for an amount no less than the amount of the unpaid principal balance of the Note (co-insurance not exceeding 80% permitted). Such insurance policy shall contain a standard mortgage clause in favor of Beneficiary and shall not be cancellable, terminable or modifiable without ten (10) days prior written notice to Beneficiary. Trustor shall promptly repair, maintain and replace the Trust Estate or any part thereof so that, except for ordinary wear and tear, the Trust Estate shall not deteriorate. In no event shall the Trustor commit waste on or to the Trust Estate.

4. ACTIONS AFFECTING TRUST ESTATE. Trustor shall appear in and contest any action or proceeding purporting to affect the security hereof or the rights or powers of Beneficiary or Trustee, and shall pay all costs and expenses, including cost of evidence of title and attorney's fees, in any such action or proceeding in which Beneficiary or Trustee may appear. Should Trustor fail to make any payment or to do any act as and in the manner provided in any of the Loan Instruments, Beneficiary and/or Trustee, each in its own discretion, without obligation so to do and without notice to or demand upon Trustor and without releasing Trustor from any obligation, may make or do the same in such manner and to such extent as either may deem necessary to protect the security hereof. Trustor shall, immediately upon demand therefor by Beneficiary, pay all costs and expenses incurred by Beneficiary in connection with the exercise by beneficiary of the foregoing rights, including without limitation costs of evidence of title, court costs, appraisals, surveys and attorney's fees. Any such costs and expenses not paid within ten (10) days of written demand shall draw interest at the default rate provided in the Note.

5. EMINENT DOMAIN. Should the Trust Estate, or any part thereof or interest therein, be taken or damaged by reason of any public improvement or condemnation proceeding, or in any other manner including deed in lieu of Condemnation ("Condemnation"), or should Trustor recive any notice or other information regarding such proceeding, Trustor shall give prompt written notice thereof to Beneficiary. Beneficiary shall be entitled to all compensation, awards and other payments or relief therefor, and shall be entitled at its option to commence, appear in and prosecute in its own name any action or proceedings. Beneficiary shall also be entitled to make any compromise or settlement in connection with such taking or damage. All such compensation, awards, damages, rights of action and proceeds awarded to Trustor (the "Proceeds") are hereby assigned to Beneficiary and Trustor agrees to execute such further assignments of the Proceeds as Beneficiary or Trustee may require.

6. APPOINTMENT OF SUCCESSOR TRUSTEE. Beneficiary may, from time to time, by a written instrument executed and acknowledged by Beneficiary, mailed to Trustor and Recorded in the County in which the Trust Estate is located and by otherwise complying with the provisions of the applicable law of the State of Nebraska substitute a successor or successors to the Trustee named herein or acting hereunder.

7. SUCCESSORS AND ASSIGNS. This Deed of Trust applies to, inures to the benefit of and binds all parties hereto, their heirs, legatees, devicees, personal representatives, successors and assigns. The term "Beneficiary" shall mean the owner and holder of the Note, whether or not named as Beneficiary herein.

8. INSPECTIONS. Beneficiary, or its agents, representatives or workmen, are authorized to enter at any reasonable time upon or in any part of the Trust Estate for the purpose of inspecting the same and for the purpose of performing any of the acts it is authorized to perform under the terms of any of the Loan Instruments.

9. EVENTS OF DEFAULT. Any of the following events shall be deemed an event of default hereunder:
(a) Trustor shall have failed to make payment of any installment of interest, principal, or principal and interest or any other sum secured hereby when due; or
(b) There has occurred a breach of or default under any term, covenant, agreement, condition, provision, representation or warranty contained in any of the Loan Instruments.

10. ACCELERATION UPON DEFAULT, ADDITIONAL REMEDIES. Should an event of default occur Beneficiary may declare all indebtedness secured hereby to be due and payable and the same shall thereupon become due and payable without any presentment, demand, protest or notice of any kind. Thereafter Beneficiary may:

(i) Either in person or by agent, with or without bringing any action or proceeding, or by a receiver appointed by a court and without regard to the adequacy of its security, enter upon and take possession of the Trust Estate, or any part thereof, in its own name or in the name of Trustee, and do any acts which it deems necessary or desirable to preserve the value, marketability or rentability of the Trust Estate, or part thereof or interest therein, increase the income therefrom or protect the security hereof and, with or without taking possession of the Trust Estate, sue for or otherwise collect the rents, issues and profits thereof, including those past due and unpaid, and apply the same, less costs and expenses of operation and collection including attorneys' fees, upon any indebtedness secured hereby, all in such order as Beneficiary may determine. The entering upon and taking possession of the Trust Estate, the collection of such rents, issues and profits and the application thereof as aforesaid, shall not cure or waive any default or notice of default hereunder or invalidate any act done in response to such default or pursuant to such notice of default and, notwithstanding the continuance in possession of the Trust Estate or the collection, receipt and application of rents, issues or profits, Trustee or Beneficiary shall be entitled to exercise every right provided for in any of the Loan Instruments or by law upon occurrence of any event of default, including the right to exercise the power of sale;

(ii) Commence an action to foreclose this Deed of Trust as a mortgage, appoint a receiver, or specifically enforce any of the covenants hereof;

(iii) Deliver to Trustee a written declaration of default and demand for sale, and a written notice of default and election to cause Trustor's interest in the Trust Estate to be sold, which notice Trustee shall cause to be duly filed for record in the appropriate Official Records of the County in which the Trust Estate is located.

11. FORECLOSURE BY POWER OF SALE. Should Beneficiary elect to foreclose by exercise of the Power of Sale herein contained, Beneficiary shall notify Trustee and shall deposit with Trustee this Deed of Trust and the Note and such receipts and evidence of expenditures made and secured hereby as Trustee may require.

(a) Upon receipt of such notice from Beneficiary, Trustee shall cause to be recorded, published and delivered to Trustor such Notice of Default and Notice of Sale as then required by law and by this Deed of Trust. Trustee shall, without demand on Trustor, after such time as may then be required by law and after recordation of such Notice of Default and after Notice of Sale having been given as required by law, sell the Trust Estate at the time and place of sale fixed by it in such Notice of Sale, either as a whole, or in separate lots or parcels or items as Trustee shall deem expedient, and in such order as it may determine, at public auction to the highest bidder for cash in lawful money of the United States payable at the time of sale. Trustee shall deliver to such purchaser or purchasers thereof its good and sufficient deed of deeds conveying the property so sold, but without any covenant or warranty, express or implied. The recitals in such deed of any matters or facts shall be conclusive proof of the truthfulness thereof. Any person, including, without limitation, Trustor, Trustee and Beneficiary, may purchase at such sale and Trustor hereby covenants to warrant and defend the title of such purchaser or purchasers.

(b) As may be permitted by law, after deducting all costs, fees and expenses of Trustee and of this Trust, including costs of evidence of title in connection with sale, Trustee shall apply the proceeds of sale to payment of (i) all sums expended under the terms hereof, not then repaid, with accrued interest at ____ percent (____%) per annum, (ii) all other sums then secured hereby, and (iii) the remainder, if any, to the person or persons legally entitled thereto.

(c) Trustee may in the manner provided by law, postpone sale of all or any portion of the Trust Estate.

12. REMEDIES NOT EXCLUSIVE. Trustee and Beneficiary, and each of them, shall be entitled to enforce payment and performance of any indebtedness or obligations secured hereby and to exercise all rights and powers under this Deed of Trust or under any Loan Instrument or other agreement or any laws now or hereafter in force, notwithstanding some or all of the such indebtedness and obligations secured hereby may now or hereafter be otherwise secured, whether by mortgage, deed of trust, pledge, lien, assignment or otherwise. Neither the acceptance of this Deed of Trust nor its enforcement whether

by court action or pursuant to the power of sale or other powers herein contained, shall prejudice or in any manner affect Trustee's or Beneficiary's right to realize upon or enforce any other security now or hereafter held by Trustee or Beneficiary, it being agreed that Trustee and Beneficiary, and each of them, shall be entitled to enforce this Deed of Trust and any other security now or hereafter held by Beneficiary or Trustee in such order and manner as they or either of them may in their absolute discretion determine. No remedy herein conferred upon or reserved to Trustee or Beneficiary is intended to be exclusive of any other remedy herein or by law provided or permitted, but each shall be cumulative and shall be in addition to every other remedy given hereunder or now or hereafter existing at law or in equity or by statute. Every power or remedy given by any of the Loan Instruments to Trustee or Beneficiary or to which either of them may be otherwise entitled, may be exercised, concurrently or independently, from time to time and as often as may be deemed expedient by Trustee or Beneficiary and either of them may pursue inconsistent remedies. Nothing herein shall be construed as prohibiting Beneficiary from seeking a deficiency judgment against the Trustor to the extent such action is permittd by law.

REQUEST FOR NOTICE. Trustor hereby requests a copy of any notice of default and that any notice of sale hereunder be mailed to it at the address set forth in the first paragraph of this Deed of Trust.

14. GOVERNING LAW. This Deed of Trust shall be governed by the laws of the State of Nebraska. In the event that any provision or clause of any of the Loan Instruments conflicts with applicable laws, such conflicts shall not affect other provisions of such Loan Instruments which can be given effect without the conflicting provision, and to this end the provisions of the Loan Instruments are declared to be severable. This instrument cannot be waived, changed, discharged or terminated orally, but only by an instrument in writing signed by the party against whom enforcement of any waiver, change, discharge or termination is sought.

15. RECONVEYANCE BY TRUSTEE. Upon written request of Beneficiary stating that all sums secured hereby have been paid, and upon surrender of this Deed of Trust and the Note to Trustee for cancellation and retention and upon payment by Trustor of Trustee's fees, Trustee shall reconvey to Trustor, or the person or persons legally entitled thereto, without warranty, any portion of the Trust Estate then held hereunder. The recitals in such reconveyance of any matters or facts shall be conclusive proof of the truthfulness thereof. The grantee in any reconveyance may be described as "the person or persons legally entitled thereto".

16. NOTICES. Whenever Beneficiary, Trustor or Trustee shall desire to give or serve any notice, demand, request or other communication with respect to this Deed of Trust, each such notice, demand, request or other communication shall be in writing and shall be effective only if the same is delivered by personal service or mailed by certified mail, postage prepaid, return receipt requested, addressed to the address set forth at the beginning of this Deed of Trust. Any party may at this time change its address for such notices by delivering or mailing to the other parties hereto, as aforesaid, a notice of such change.

17. ACCEPTANCE BY TRUSTEE. Trustee accepts this Trust when this Deed of Trust, duly executed and acknowledged, is made a public record as provided by law.

IN WITNESS WHEREOF, Trustor has executed this Deed of Trust as of the day and year first above written. TRUSTEE. Trustee accepts this Trust when this Deed of Trust, duly executed and acknowledged, is made a public record as provided by law.

IN WITNESS WHEREOF, Trustor has executed this Deed of Trust as of the day and year first above written.

SELLER'S SETTLEMENT SHEET

Date _____

Name of Seller _____

Address _____

Property _____

	Debit	Credit
Sale price	$	$_____
Earnest money, per sale agreement	_____	
Additional payment received prior to date of this statement	_____	
Contract amount carried back by seller	_____	
Existing mortgage	_____	
Rebate of escrow fund		_____
Pro-rated insurance—unearned premium		_____
Pro-rated real estate taxes—general	_____	
Pro-rated real estate taxes—special	_____	
Interest adjustment	_____	_____
Pro-rated rent	_____	
Recording fees—Release of mortgage	_____	
Affidavit	_____	
Abstracting	_____	
Land survey	_____	
Appraisal fee	_____	
Attorney's fees	_____	
Revenue stamps	_____	
Commission	_____	
_____		
_____		
Debit balance buyer	_____	
TOTALS	$_____	$_____

Remarks _____

Duplicate, original received, read, and approved.

_____   _____
Seller   Broker

_____   _____
Seller   By

BUYER'S SETTLEMENT SHEET

Date _____

Name of Buyer _____

Address _____

Property _____

	Debit	Credit
Purchase price	$_____	$
Earnest money paid with signing of purchase agreement		_____
Additional payment made prior to date of this statement		_____
To reimburse broker for earnest money advanced		_____
Old mortgage assumed		_____
New mortgage		_____
Contract with seller		_____
Loan closing costs	_____	
Pro-rated insurance, or new insurance premium	_____	
Pro-rated real estate taxes—general		_____
Pro-rated real estate taxes—special		_____
Pro-rated rent		_____
Replacement, or new escrow fund deposited with mortgage holder	_____	
Interest adjustment	_____	_____
Tax adjustment	_____	
Recording fees	_____	
Abstracting	_____	
Appraisal fee	_____	
Attorney's fee	_____	
Credit report	_____	
Credit balance seller		_____
TOTALS	$_____	$_____

Remarks _____

Duplicate, original received, read, and approved.

_____ Seller   _____ Broker

_____ Seller   _____ By

A. Settlement Statement

U.S. Department of Housing
and Urban Development

OMB No. 2502-0265 (Exp. 12-31-86)

B. Type of Loan

1. ☐ FHA 2. ☐ FmHA 3. ☒ Conv. Unins.	6. File Number	7. Loan Number	8. Mortgage Insurance Case Number
4. ☐ VA 5. ☐ Conv. Ins.	123456RC	2-6359412	

C. Note: This form is furnished to give you a statement of actual settlement costs. Amounts paid to and by the settlement agent are shown. Items marked "(p.o.c.)" were paid outside the closing; they are shown here for informational purposes and are not included in the totals.

D. Name and Address of Borrower	E. Name and Address of Seller	F. Name and Address of Lender
Robert C. Moore Patricia H. Moore 850 Exeter Avenue San Carlos, CA. 94070	John Jones Mary Jones 767 N. Main Street Redwood City, CA. 94063	American Financial Corporation 5653 Walnut Street, San Francisco, CA

G. Property Location	H. Settlement Agent
850 Exeter Avenue San Carlos, CA. 94070	First American Title Insurance Company

	Place of Settlement	I. Settlement Date
	555 Marshall Street Redwood City, CA 94063	5/08/90

J. Summary of Borrower's Transaction		K. Summary of Seller's Transaction	
100. Gross Amount Due From Borrower		**400. Gross Amount Due To Seller**	
101. Contract sales price	360,000.00	401. Contract sales price	360,000.00
102. Personal property		402. Personal property	
103. Settlement charges to borrower (line 1400)	8,456.50	403.	
104.		404.	
105.		405.	
Adjustments for items paid by seller in advance		*Adjustments for items paid by seller in advance*	
106. City/town taxes to		406. City/town taxes to	
107. County taxes 1/01/90 to 5/08/90	1,579.88	407. County taxes 1/01/90 to 5/08/90	1,579.88
108. Assessments to		408. Assessments to	
109.		409.	
110.		410.	
111.		411.	
112.		412.	
120. Gross Amount Due From Borrower	370,036.38	**420. Gross Amount Due To Seller**	361,579.88
200. Amounts Paid By Or In Behalf Of Borrower		**500. Reductions In Amount Due To Seller**	
201. Deposit or earnest money	63,786.38	501. Excess deposit (see instructions)	
202. Principal amount of new loan(s)	266,250.00	502. Settlement charges to seller (line 1400)	23,040.00
203. Existing loan(s) taken subject to		503. Existing loan(s) taken subject to	
204.		504. Payoff of first mortgage loan	106,341.52
205.		505. Payoff of second mortgage loan	
206.		506.	
207.		507.	
208. Second Deed of Trust	40,000.00	508. Second Deed of Trust	40,000.00
209.		509.	
Adjustments for items unpaid by seller		*Adjustments for items unpaid by seller*	
210. City/town taxes to		510. City/town taxes to	
211. County taxes to		511. County taxes to	
212. Assessments to		512. Assessments to	
213.		513.	
214.		514.	
215.		515.	
216.		516.	
217.		517.	
218.		518.	
219.		519.	
220. Total Paid By/For Borrower	370,036.38	**520. Total Reduction Amount Due Seller**	169,381.52
300. Cash At Settlement From/To Borrower		**600. Cash At Settlement To/From Seller**	
301. Gross Amount due from borrower (line 120)	370,036.38	601. Gross amount due to seller (line 420)	361,579.88
302. Less amounts paid by/for borrower (line 220)	370,036.38	602. Less reductions in amt. due seller (line 520)	(169,381.52)
303. Cash ☐ From ☒ To Borrower		603. Cash ☒ To ☐ From Seller	192,198.36

L. Settlement Charges

700. Total Sales/Broker's Commission based on price $60,000.00 @ 6.00 % =			Paid From Borrowers Funds at Settlement	Paid From Seller's Funds at Settlement
Division of Commission (line 700) as follows:				
701. $ 10,800.00	to	Smith Realty		
702. $ 10,800.00	to	Fellow Realty		
703. Commission paid at Settlement				21,600.00
704.				
800. Items Payable In Connection With Loan				
801. Loan Origination Fee %		American Financial Corporation	3,993.75	
802. Loan Discount %				
803. Appraisal Fee	to	American Financial Corporation	175.00	
804. Credit Report	to	American Financial Corporation	50.00	
805. Lender's Inspection Fee				
806. Mortgage Insurance Application Fee to				
807. Assumption Fee				
808. Tax Service		American Financial Corporation	60.50	
809. Processing Fee		American Financial Corporation	250.00	
810. Document Fee		American Financial Corporation	75.00	
811.				
900. Items Required By Lender To Be Paid In Advance				
901. Interest from 5/07/90 to 6/01/90 @ $4.69000 /day			1,367.25	
902. Mortgage Insurance Premium for months to				
903. Hazard Insurance Premium for 1 years to Farmers Ins			583.00	
904. years to				
905.				
1000. Reserves Deposited With Lender				
1001. Hazard insurance months @ $ per month				
1002. Mortgage insurance months @ $ per month				
1003. City property taxes months @ $ per month				
1004. County property taxes months @ $ per month				
1005. Annual assessments months @ $ per month				
1006. months @ $ per month				
1007. months @ $ per month				
1008. months @ $ per month				
1100. Title Charges				
1101. Settlement or closing fee	to	First American Title Ins. Co.	587.00	
1102. Abstract or title search	to			
1103. Title examination	to			
1104. Title insurance binder	to			
1105. Document preparation	to	First American Title Ins. Co.	25.00	10.00
1106. Notary fees	to	First American Title Ins. Co.	10.00	10.00
1107. Attorney's fees	to			
(includes above items numbers:)				
1108. Title insurance	to	First American Title Ins. Co.	1,260.00	
(includes above items numbers:)				
1109. Lender's coverage $ 266,250.00				
1110. Owner's coverage $ 360,000.00				
1111.				
1112.				
1113.				
1200. Government Recording and Transfer Charges				
1201. Recording fees: Deed $ 7.00 ; Mortgage $ 20.00 ; Releases $ 7.00			20.00	14.00
1202. City/county/stamps: Deed $ 396.00 ; Mortgage $ 0.00				396.00
1203. State tax/stamps: Deed $; Mortgage $				
1204.				
1205.				
1300. Additional Settlement Charges				
1301. Survey to				
1302. Pest inspection to		Moody Pest Control		135.00
1303. Pest Repairs		Moody Pest Control		875.00
1304.				
1305.				
1400. Total Settlement Charges (enter on lines 103, Section J and 502, Section K)			8,456.50	23,040.00

AGREEMENT TO OCCUPY PRIOR TO FINAL CLOSING

The undersigned Seller and Purchaser, having executed a Purchase Agreement dated _____ relating to the property located at:

Address _____

Legal Description _____

_____

and Purchaser, desiring to enter into possession of said premises prior to closing the sale and obtaining title thereto, the parties agree as follows:

1. In consideration of Seller's permission to Purchaser to take possession of the premises, Purchaser agrees:

> a. To accept the premises in its present condition.
> b. To take responsibility for and maintain heating, sewer, plumbing, and electrical systems and any built-in appliances and equipment in normal working order, to keep the roof watertight and to maintain the grounds.
> c. To have all utilities put in the name of the purchaser by the date of possession.
> d. To refrain from undertaking any alterations without prior written consent from the Seller.
> e. To abide by all laws and governmental regulations with respect to the use or occupancy of the premises.
> f. To admit Seller, or his authorized agent, at reasonable times for the purpose of inspecting the premises until the final closing.
> g. To obtain and keep a homeowner's insurance policy in the name of the purchaser in effect for the entire time of occupancy before closing. Said insurance policy to be in the amount of $_____.
>
> **Note:** Possession of the Property by the Purchaser changes policy rights. Both Purchaser and Seller should consult their insurance agent prior to initial early occupancy date.

2. This agreement is not intended to create a relationship of landlord and tenant and the right of the Purchaser to occupy the premises shall be on a day to day basis, at _____ per diem. It is agreed that _____ will be paid in advance as per the terms of this agreement or the purchase agreement, or in the event the purchaser breaches either agreement, Purchaser agrees to vacate the premises within three days following written demand by Seller, personally delivered or mailed to the premises. Purchaser agrees to pay all cost of any legal action that may be instituted by Seller to enforce the terms hereof or for the eviction of the Purchaser from the property, including a reasonable attorney's fee.

3. Purchaser will pay any reasonable costs to restore the premises to the same condition as when the Purchaser took possession should the sale not close. The Purchaser acknowledges that if a sale should not take place that the retention of possession could seriously interfere with the subsequent sale of the property and that this agreement does not cause either party to waive their right to damages should the property sale not close.

4. Early occupancy per diem charges will commence on the _____ day of _____, 19_____, and will terminate on the day of closing.

5. Occupancy date to be _____.

_____	_____
Seller	Purchaser
_____	_____
Seller	Purchaser
_____	_____
Date	Date
Subscribed and sworn to me	Subscribed and sworn to me
on this _____ day of	on this _____ day of
_____, 19_____	_____, 19_____
_____	_____
Notary Public	Notary Public

CONSTRUCTION LIEN

1. This real estate subject to this lien is: _____
_____

2. The person against whose interest in the real estate the lien is claimed is: _____
_____

3. The name and address of the claimant are: _____
_____

4. The name and address of the person with whom the claimant contracted is: _____
_____

5. A general description of the claimant's services performed to, to be performed or materials furnished or to be furnished for the improvement and the contract price is: _____
_____
_____

6. (Complete one of the following)
___ The amount unpaid, whether due or not, to the claimant for the services or materials is
$_____.
___ The unpaid amount is not fixed by the contract, but a good faith estimate in the amount of
$_____.

7. (Complete one of the following)
___ The time the last services or materials were furnished was _____.
___ The time the last services or materials were furnished has not yet occurred but is estimated to occur
_____.

_____
Signature of Claimant

Index